Making Peace with Your Past

One Choice at a Time

Cindy Hyde

This book is dedicated to everyone with a past

and to my wonderful husband who lets me be me.
Thank you Michael Hyde. You are amazing.

Scripture quotations marked KJV are from the Holy Bible, King James Version.

Scripture quotations marked NIV are from the Holy Bible, New International Version®, NIV® Copyright © 1973, 1978, 1984, 2011 by Biblica, Inc.® Used by permission. All rights reserved worldwide.

Scripture quotations marked NLT are taken from the Holy Bible, New Living Translation, copyright ©1996, 2004, 2007. Used by permission of Tyndale House Publishers, Inc., Carol Stream, Illinois 60188. All Rights Reserved.

Subject Headings: CHURCH WORK WITH THE HURTING / EMOTIONAL ABUSE / EMOTIONAL HEALING / COUNSELING / SELF-HELP

ISBN: 9780692460238

About the Author

Cindy Hyde, M.A.Ed. was born in Harrisonville, MO and moved to Texas.

Cindy is a published author, teacher, speaker, and ordained minister. She has been in full-time ministry for more than 21 years. She is a Faith-based Pastoral Counselor and a Certified Professional Life Coach. She has served as a Certified Chaplain through the Community of Hope, a branch of St. Luke's Hospital. She is also a Certified Divine Healing Technician through John G. Lake Ministries.

Cindy is the CEO/Founder of the East Texas Healing Center, a faith-based 501(c)3 religious organization established as a hospital for the soul helping those affected by crisis. She started the Healing Center in 2002 and since that time hundreds of people have experienced the power of the Gospel of Jesus Christ that brings comfort, healing, restoration, reconciliation, peace, and abundant life.

Cindy passionately shares the love of the Father, and truths about healing from God's Word. Wounded hearts are healed, captives are set free, relationships are reconciled, and God ordained identities are restored. Cindy draws from her life experiences, her knowledge of the Scripture, and wisdom to help others make peace with their past one choice at a time.

Cindy and her husband Michael have four (six counting their son-in-law and a daughter-in-law, 11 grandchildren, and a new great-granddaughter, oh, and a four-legged fur-child, a Poodle named Quincy. They have lived in Nacogdoches since 1993. They serve together in ministry and enjoy dining out and watching movies.

Introduction

Everyone has a past. There are many things that happen to us in our lifetime. Parents are not perfect. Children are not perfect. They make mistakes. We make mistakes. We enter into relationships that are not perfect because we are imperfect ourselves. Relationships can cause heartache when there is abuse involved. There are many types of abuse: sexual, verbal, financial, physical, mental, and emotional. Abuse leaves soul wounds. These wounds must be healed. The Lord Christ Jesus came to heal the brokenhearted. He is our Healer. Not only will He heal you, He will reveal to you true and unconditional love. He will restore your joy and give you peace.

Through the power of the Gospel, the sacred blood of Jesus Christ, the life-changing Word of God, and the guidance of the Holy Spirit, you will make peace with your past. Staying wounded, bitter, resentful, broken, or angry is your option. An unhealthy one, but it is still a choice you must make.

If you choose to allow the Lord to help, you will make peace with your past, you will become who you were created to be, and you will be able to love and be loved. If you choose to stay wounded and angry you will continue to live in pain, misery, and heartache. Again it is a choice you must make. The Lord wants to heal every area of your life. He does not want you broken, shattered, or even cracked. He does not want you wounded and hurting. He wants to make you whole. He wants you to be happy, peaceful, and successful.

If you are out of balance emotionally, if you struggle with past traumatic events that left you fearful, feeling guilt, shame, or condemnation, there is hope and there is help. You do not have to allow your past to continue robbing you of your future.

As you work through the pages of this workbook, you will discover several methods for making peace with your past. When you make the choice to move in the direction of healing, the Lord will meet you where you are.

It is my hope and my prayer, that the words and exercises in this workbook will guide you one choice closer to finding the type of peace that passes understanding. You are worth it.

Table of Contents

Course Description, Goals and Objectives

Course Description

In this course, you will be introduced to God's personal message of love, hope, and healing. You will be challenged to look at your own life and apply the principles of grace and forgiveness to yourself and others. You will learn to make peace with your past one choice at a time.

Course Goal

The goal of this course is to provide you several different ways of dealing or coping with the painful memories, the traumatic events, and the disappointments you have experienced in your life so you can live a life filled with love, joy, and peace.

Learning Objectives

At the end of this course you will:

1. Realize why you were created and what you were created for.
2. Establish your identity and realize your true value.
3. Recognize both the negative and positive events throughout your life and the impact they have had in your daily choices.
4. Distinguish between healthy and unhealthy thoughts.
5. Understand what forgiveness is and experience it for yourself and forgive others.
6. Understand the true meaning of love and begin expressing and receiving love in a healthy way.
7. Know the difference between functional and dysfunctional relationships.
8. Understand how your beliefs impact your emotional health and behaviors.
9. Develop healthy coping skills like how to make choices and manage stress.
10. Know how to resolve conflicts and communicate effectively.

Making Peace with Your Past
One Choice at a Time

Cindy Hyde

Chapter One

God's Plan and Your Purpose

You Can Choose to Discover God's Plan for Your Life

Have you ever asked yourself questions like these?

- Who is God?

- Why am I here?

- What is my purpose?

- Isn't there more to life than what I have?

Questions like these do have answers. You may not have those answers right now but I am sure you will have more answers by the time you finish this workbook than you do right now.

You may not realize this but God has a plan. He has always had a plan. He always will. You are part of His plan. Yes you. Why not you? Part of His plan was to create you for Himself. He created you for love. He created you to love and to be loved. Love is one of the main things the enemy of our souls (our advisory, the one who is against us) works the hardest to distort in our lives. God is Love. If the enemy of our soul can distort your idea, concept, reality, or belief system about love then he has accomplished his goal of hindering your relationship with Love itself.

He did not create you without purpose so you would have to flounder through life without direction. You have a Divine destiny. He has a Divine plan for your life. Once you begin exchanging some of your beliefs you will begin changing your core identity. Once you do that you will realize what a valuable treasure you are. As you read this chapter God's plan for humanity (you) will become clearer, as will your created purpose.

How Do You Describe God?

1. Is God active in my life?

2. Do I trust God?

3. Do I ever feel joy in my relationship with God?

4. Do I ever feel a strong sense of belonging to God?

5. Do I clearly know right from wrong?

6. Do I know what God wants from me?

7. On a scale of 1-10, how would I rate my faith in God?

8. Which of my actions show rebellion towards God or bring Him glory?

9. Do I pray?

10. Do I believe God forgives my mistakes?

11. What do I give to God?

12. What does God give to me?

God has a plan.

Why We Were Created
(Retrieved and used with permission from http://www.whywewerecreated.com)

God's Plan

Our existence is not the result of some random series of biological accidents that occurred a long time ago. We were intentionally created by a loving Creator who gave us His gift of life. (1)

It is not because of the well-meaning intentions of our parents that we exist. Each one of us is here today because we originated in the heart of the Father of our spirit before the earth was formed. (2)

Our lives have true meaning because we are the workmanship of a tenderhearted Father whose royal plan for us dates back to the creation of humanity's first couple... Adam and Eve. (3)

It was Almighty God who intimately knew us and planned our coronation into humanity, even before we were conceived. (4) Though our parents played their part, it was our loving Creator who knit us together in our mother's womb (5) and welcomed us into this world on the day we were born. (6)

All of creation was thrilled with our arrival because from heaven's perspective, we are known as the offspring of God. (7) It was God who determined when we would be born and He chose where we would live. (8)

Because we were created in God's own image, (9) our value to Him is beyond anything that we could possibly measure with our human understanding. (10) He planned every day of our lives (11) and He even took the time to number every hair on our heads. (12) Though we may not acknowledge God, He acknowledges us and He loves us with an everlasting love. (13)

The angels know who we are and it is their mission is to help us fulfill our divine purpose. (14) The demons know who we are and it is their intent to deceive us and to steal what is rightfully ours. (15) This battle has been raging over humanity ever since the Garden of Eden (16) and it continues to war over every person on the planet today. (17)

The Brokenness of Humanity

Because of our fallen humanity, (18) we have been caught in a downward spiral of despair and disillusionment. (19) Though we have been separated from God, He has not been separated from us (20) for the Bible says that 'in Him we live and move and have our being'. (21)

In our ignorance, some of us have created theories that eliminate His existence and have thus nullified our own divine origin. While others, in their misguided efforts to be self-righteous, have invented false ways to become enlightened apart from the one and only path that truly leads to God. (22)

Instead of recognizing and valuing the reflection of God that each human being carries, we have disregarded His image and hurt what He loves... and that is each other. The result has been the perpetuation of a cycle of pain and suffering that has been passed on from one generation to the next.

Over the centuries, we have seen progress as a way to better ourselves, only to see tyranny and greed increase with it, causing further abuse to ourselves and to our planet. In our own effort to be good apart from God, we have strayed even further away from Eden than ever before. With each attempt to find ourselves, we have become even more lost. (23)

God's Restoration

But God has never given up on the dream He has for us. (24) He was, and is, and always will be, committed to seeing what was stolen in the Garden, fully restored. (25)

That is why two thousand years ago, He fulfilled a plan that was hatched even before the creation of the world. (26) He sent His only Son to the earth so that He could become our way back home. (27) It was for this purpose that Jesus Christ, the Son of the living God became like one of us... fully man, yet fully God, and did what no other person in history could ever do. (28)

Jesus took upon Himself all of our brokenness so that we could be completely set free from all of the consequences of our own sinfulness. (29) The Son of God exchanged His divine life for our broken life when He died on a cross (30) so that we could be forgiven and reconciled to His Father. (31)

When Jesus rose from the grave, (32) He destroyed the power of death and sin forever! (33) Through His once and for all sacrifice, (34) we now have a clear pathway back to God (35) and to complete restoration of our divine purpose. (36)

Through our creation, we became God's offspring. (37) But through our Heavenly Father's plan of redemption, we can now become His full-fledged children (38) by being born anew into His Kingdom. (39) If we just reach out our hand, we will find Him because He is not far from us. (40)

Our Created Purpose

We were created to live forever (41) and enjoy the vast inheritance that our God and Father has stored up for us in heaven. (42) This is our spiritual destiny and what God intended all along. (43) For we are His masterpiece, created to do the amazing works that He prepared for us to do. (44)

This is not a fairy tale or something that is too good to be true. We are not a mistake or the result of some random, impersonal, mathematically impossible, biological uncertainty.

We are all the image bearers of Almighty God! (45) We were created to be loved by the One who is love itself (46) and purposed by Him to belong to His everlasting family. (47) It is our Father's heart that we recognize our true created purpose (48) and come home to the love we have been looking for all our lives. (49) It is time for us to receive our royal position in the Kingdom of God (50) and take our rightful place at His table. (51) Jesus Christ has secured the way for us to fulfill our destiny as children of the Most High. (52)

By receiving Jesus, (53) we are restored to the dignity and glory that Almighty God intended for us from the very beginning. (54) All creation is waiting for us to experience our God-ordained birthright. (55)

All we have to do is to simply believe it to be true and yield to our Heavenly Father's eternal plan, freely given to us through His beloved Son, Jesus Christ. (56) (Father Heart Communication, 2013)

Bible References

(1) Genesis 2:7; (2) Isaiah 64:8; (3) Genesis 2:21-25; (4) Jeremiah 1:4-5; (5) Psalm 139:13; (6) Psalm 71:6; (7) Acts 17:28; (8) Acts 17:26; (9) Genesis 1:27; (10) Romans 8:31-32; (11) Psalm 139:16; (12) Matthew 10:29-31; (13) Jeremiah 31:3; (14) Hebrews 1:14; (15) 1 Peter 5:8; (16) Genesis 3; (17) Ephesians 6:11-12; (18) Romans 5:12; (19) Isaiah 53:6; (20) Acts 17:27; (21) Acts 17:28; (22) Romans 1:21-23; (23) Romans 3:23; (24) 2 Peter 3:9; (25) John 10:10; (26) Revelation 13:8; (27) John 3:16; (28) Philippians 2:5-11; (29) 2 Corinthians 5:21; (30) Colossians 2:13-15; (31) 2 Corinthians 5:18-19; (32) Luke 24; (33) Romans 8:1-2; (34) Hebrews 10:10; (35) John 14:6; (36) Romans 8:15-17; (37) Acts 17:28; (38) Ephesians 1:3-10; (39) 2 Corinthians 5:17; (40) Acts 17:27; (41) John 6:51; (42) 1 Peter 1:3-5; (43) Psalm 8:4-6; (44) Ephesians 2:10, (45) Genesis 1:26; (46) 1 John 4:16; (47) Ephesians 3:14-15; (48) Romans 8:29; (49) John 14:1-3; (50) Galatians 4:4-7; (51) Revelation 21:1-4; (52) Ephesians 1:11-23; (53) John 1:12-13 (54) Hebrews 2:9-11; (55) Romans 8:19 (56) Romans 10:9

Chapter Two

Your Identity and Worth

You Can Choose to Start Believing You are Worthy

Think about the following questions.

- How do I define self-esteem, self-value or self-worth?

- How valuable do I think I am I right now?

- What is my esteem, value or worth based on?

- Do other people determine my worth?

- How has my identity been established?

What is Self-Esteem?

The term self-esteem is defined by a person's sense of self-worth or personal value. Self-esteem, self-worth, and self-value are all interchangeable words to describe the same thing. The beliefs we have about our self or the opinion we have about our appearance, our actions, and even our own belief systems determine our level of self-esteem.

In other words if you think highly of yourself, if you think or believe you are valuable or that you have worth you will take care of yourself, you will not do things that harm your body or that harm others, you normally make decisions that cause you to end up in good situations.

If you believe you are not valuable you may end up in dead-end or abusive relationships. You might not think you can do anything right or that everything you do is wrong. You may put yourself down and have negative thoughts about yourself. You might even believe you deserve to be punished because you are such a bad person. Let me tell you something, and this is truth: There is no such thing as a bad person. People are not good or bad. We make bad choices which cause bad results, but God created us and saw what He created, "And God saw everything that he had made, and, behold, it was very good." Gen. 1:31 KJV

God did not create people in His image to be bad. There are people who make more bad choices than others. I am thankful that we are not what we do. We do however; become a product of our bad choices. We can have bad habits and those lead to bad consequences. The price a person pays for their bad choices and bad habits are always high, even to the loss of their freedom, their health, and even their life. You can never get positive results from negative decisions.

Bad habits bring about bad results and they need to be exchanged. To change a habit it simply needs to be replaced with another one. In fact, it only takes 21 days to form a new habit. We need to rewire our thinking to get the negative out of our lives and exchange them for healthier choices.

If you believe you are valuable your emotions and your actions will be evident and they will speak loudly. Your actions and your emotions will always let others know what you think you are worth. People with a high self-esteem are noticeable. They are usually successful in life even if they fail at times.

Your self-esteem should not be low or high. Those with a very high self-esteem are usually narcissistic. Meaning they think about themselves, what they want, and how to get what they want more than thinking about anyone else. In other words, their world revolves around them. People with a low self-esteem are of often co-dependents. Meaning they care more for others and take better care of others than they do themselves, often neglecting themselves for the sake of others even if it is not asked or demanded of them.

"We are cruel to ourselves. We try to live in this world without knowing about the God Whose world it is and Who runs it. The world becomes a strange, mad, painful place and life in it a disappointing and unpleasant business, for those who do not know about God. Disregard the study of God, and you sentence yourself to stumble and blunder through life blindfolded, as it were, with no sense of direction and no understanding of what surrounds you. In this way you can waste your life and lose your soul." - J.I. Packer (Knowing God)

What Are You Really Worth?

God places a higher value on us than we place on ourselves. Actually, the value of a human body in terms of our chemical and mineral composition is surprising. Demand Media (2010) stated, "A great number of people have spent a great deal of human and financial resources calculating the composition of, prior to the decomposition of, and the worth, or worthlessness of, the human body." They also state that "When we total the monetary value of the elements in our bodies and the value of the average person's skin, we arrive at a net worth of $4.50!"

Your Net Worth

$4.50!

According to Demand Media (2010), the "U.S. Bureau of Chemistry and Soils invested many a hard-earned tax dollar in calculating the chemical and mineral composition of the human body, which breaks down as follows:

65% Oxygen	3% Nitrogen	0.00004% Iodine	0.35% Potassium
18% Carbon	0.25% Sulfur	1.5% Calcium	0.15% Chlorine
10% Hydrogen	0.15% Sodium	1% Phosphorous	0.05% Magnesium
			0.0004% Iron

Note: As you can see, we have little value as a physical human. Our value must come from the One who created us. When we understand who we are to our Creator, our Heavenly Father, we can develop a healthy self-esteem. The Bible paints a clear picture of our worth. On the next page is a partial list of Scriptures that help us understand our value and worth in our Father's eyes.

Self Esteem Quiz

A quiz for self-esteem is a way for you to determine how you see yourself. By being honest with yourself as to where you are today, you can see where you need to make improvements. Your self-image is how you evaluate your own life, how you feel about your job, your relationships and where you're going.

How do you really feel about yourself? Do you have a harsh, negative opinion of yourself? Find out what kind of self-image you have by taking the quiz for self-esteem below.

For each question, choose one of the following answers. The number next to the answer represents how many points that answer is worth. Total your scores and check on your results below;

1 – Never
2 – Rarely
3 – Sometimes
4 – Usually
5 – Always

Questions

_____1. You express your opinions openly.

_____2. You have no fear of being rejected by other people

_____3. When you have to make a major decision that affects mostly you (such as changing jobs), you may consult with other people, but the final decision is your own.

_____4. You forgive yourself for your mistakes.

_____5. You believe you deserve the best life has to offer.

_____6. You accept yourself for being the way you are.

_____7. You are able to express your feelings, both positive and negative.

_____8. You set aside some time just for you.

_____9. You ask for help when you need it.

_____10. You will return an unsatisfactory item to a store.

_____11. You don't worry about what others think of you.

_____12. If you are dissatisfied with an important part of your life, you will take steps to make a change.

_____13. You are comfortable making eye contact with other people.

_____14. When criticized, you listen, but don't take it personally.

_____15. You are comfortable trying new things.

_____16. You can make a list of your accomplishments and/or positive qualities without a great deal of difficulty.

_____17. You are comfortable around successful people.

_____18. You believe you can handle anything.

What your scores on the quiz for self-esteem mean?

0 – 18: Time to Change
You question every decision you make and are crippled by lack of self-respect. Your self-esteem is dangerously low and you MUST make improving your self-esteem a #1 priority in your life.

19–36: Signs of Trouble
You believe other people are worth more than you are. Your self-esteem is shaky at best and needs work.

37-54: Middle of the Road
You have days when you think you're doing ok, and days when you question everything you do. Work on believing in yourself a little more, and everything will fall into place.

55-72: On the right track
Your faith in yourself is on the right track, but can use improvement. Practice recognizing each small accomplishment and your self-esteem will start to soar.

73-90: Solid self-esteem
No one has to tell you that you're ok! You have a healthy sense of self-respect and rarely, if ever, question your decisions. You learn from your mistakes instead of dwelling on them. Keep up the good work!

People with self-esteem:
This next section was retrieved from www.selfesteem2go.com.

• ENJOY LIFE. If you understand and practice this, you don't even have to read any further. Just keep it doing. This is the most important part of our well-being. This is the factor what people are willing to forget about. Very simple yet very powerful. So be it. Live your life.

• JUST DO IT. They are always in action. They do it whether they like it or not, because they know that action takes you to the next level. Whenever you accomplish something that gives you the feeling of satisfaction that is what raises the level of your self-esteem.

• Have OPTIMISM, which gives the fuel to the engine to start working. Positive thinking is one of the most important factors for developing self-esteem, to begin to change your life for goods.

• RESPECT themselves and others. What you give out, that's what you get back. Respect will determine your social status as well. People need to engage in certain activities – profession, hobby, others – to gain recognition and to feel accepted and self-valued. However, to respect yourself, you have to THINK INDEPENDENTLY and not waiting for outside recognition to feel good about yourself. The acknowledgements of others should only be an additional trophy to your self-respect. This is crucial for developing self-esteem.

• Hold themselves worthy to be LOVED and love others. Therefore they are WORTHY OF SUCCESS.

• Have INTEGRITY. They have reasonable principles to guide their lives and they act according to it.

• TRUST their own mental ability to rise above the crowd.

• Are GOAL-ORIENTED. They set clear goals and they are moving forward achieving them. To build high self-esteem you have to have crystal clear goals to know where you are now and where you are going.

• Know how to FOCUS. They are paying attention on their priorities and eliminating the destructive patterns from their life. Focus is indispensable for developing self-esteem.

• Know the enormous power of PERSONAL DEVELOPMENT, constant learning and using that knowledge to fulfill their potential.

• Have CONTROL over their life. They realize that they are the only ones who can MAKE DECISIONS and they do that quickly if it's necessary.
    • Have a sense of HUMOR. Every smile is a miracle which can create other miracles.

• Are CREATIVE and have healthy coping skills to handle concerns and problems. Developing self-esteem is a creative process.

• Are RESPONSIBLE for their actions. They don't try to blame it on others; they are the first ones to be in charge and to take control over the situation according to their best knowledge.

• Are PERSISTENT. They are eager to accomplish their chosen goals and they have the energy, the motivation to move closer and closer even if they feel tired or lost. They never, ever give up.

This is the summary of the key "ingredients" of self-esteem. You can always add to it. You can rephrase the paragraphs. It doesn't matter. The point is that you have to put the idea, the determination and the will of change into your mind and start going toward your goals.

"YOU MAKE ZERO PERCENT OF THE SHOTS YOU DON'T TAKE."
Michael Jordan

So get out of the couch and start moving. Gets the blood going and you already feel better. Developing self-esteem is like making a soup. You have to have basic ingredients – water, vegetables, meat, pasta etc. - , but it is highly recommended to use your own style, imagination, heart to create the taste of a lifetime. You can always add a bit of a salt or pepper to it. Spice it up!

Therefore, be flexible and do not try to follow any system or help without thinking about it. Use your human judgment to set the direction of your life. Do what makes sense. I will provide you with as much information as you need to build self-esteem. Use your brain to choose the factors you feel comfortable with and do it. The reward of developing self-esteem – your overall well-being - will follow. And do not forget about one thing:

"NEVER, NEVER, NEVER, NEVER GIVE UP"
Winston Churchill

Thanks selfesteem2go.com for the great input.

You Can Choose to Stop Using Excuses

The next time you feel like God can't use you, just remember . . .

NOAH- was a drunk.

ABRAHAM- was too old.

ISAAC- was a daydreamer.

JACOB- was a liar.

JOSEPH- was abused.

MOSES- had a stuttering problem.

GIDEON- was afraid.

SAMSON- had long hair and was a womanizer.

RAHAB- was a prostitute.

JEREMIAH and TIMOTHY were too young.

DAVID was an adulterer and a murderer.

ELIJAH was suicidal.

JONAH ran from God.

NAOMI was a widow.

JOB went bankrupt.

JOHN the Baptist ate bugs.

PETER denied Christ.

THE DISCIPLES fell asleep while praying.

MARTHA worried about everything.

MARY MAGDALENE had seven unclean spirits.

THE SAMARITAN WOMAN was divorced more than once.

ZACCHEUS was very small.

PAUL was too religious.

TIMOTHY had an ulcer ... AND

LAZARUS WAS DEAD!

NOW what is YOUR EXCUSE?
Author Unknown.

Characteristics of Unhealthy and Healthy Self-esteem

Please circle all that apply to you.

1. Fear, Stress and Anxiety	1. Peace
2. Depression	2. Joy & Happiness
3. Hypersensitive, Defensiveness	3. Easy Going, Stable
4. Unhealthy Relationships	4. Healthy Relationships
5. Inadequacy	5. Adequate and Sufficient
6. Worthlessness	6. Worthy, Valuable, Significant
7. Critical	7. Praising and Complimentary
8. Self-sabotaging	8. Self-encouraging, Confident
9. Poor self-care	9. Good Self-Care
10. No boundaries (Can't say no.)	10. Healthy Boundaries
11. Passive-Aggressive behaviors	11. Healthy Expression of Emotions
12. Pessimistic, Negative Outlook	12. Optimistic, Positive Outlook
13. Poor Communication Skills	13. Good Communication Skills
14. Irresponsible	14. Responsible and Reliable
15. Disrespectful to self and others	15. Loves and accept self and others
16. Know-It-All Attitude	16. Listens and Respect Other's Opinions
17. Self-abasing (degrading)	17. Self-improving

Now give the Lord permission to work with you to bring about the changes you see need to be made. Then let Him do it.

You Can Choose to Create a Healthier Self-Esteem and Increase Your Confidence

There are several steps you can take to help you improve your self-esteem and confidence level. Here are a few of them.

1. Believe what the Word of God says about you.

2. Face your authentic self. Learn to love and accept yourself today.

3. Think only about things that are good, pure, of a good report (Phil 4:8)

4. Do a personal inventory of your strengths, skills and positive attributes.

5. Do a personal inventory of your perceived limits or weaknesses.

6. Celebrate your strengths. Realize you have a specialized skill set to offer.

7. Make a plan to improve the perceived limits or weaknesses you want to work on.

8. Make a plan to use your strengths, skills and positive attributes in helpful ways.

9. Create a plan for your life, including short-term and long-term goals.

10. Create a daily schedule and go over it every night before going to bed.

11. Realize some of your beliefs are actually lies. Confront them with the truth.

12. Think of ways you can change what you feel bad about.

13. Learn to manage the stress in your life by improving your coping skills.

14. Recognize and remove all negative self-talk (thinking) from your life.

15. Pat yourself on the back and reward yourself for all improvements.

You can build your self-esteem by choosing to work with yourself instead of against yourself.
Cindy Hyde

You Can Choose to Build a Godly Self-Worth with Scripture

Read the following Scriptures as often as you can for the next few weeks to help you retrain your mind and your heart to receive the truth about your identity and worth.

1. I AM LOVED BY GOD

    a. For God so loved the world that he gave his one and only Son, that whoever believes in him shall not perish but have eternal life. (John 3:16)

    b. This is love: not that we loved God, but the he loved us and sent his Son as an atoning sacrifice for our sins. (1 John 4:10)

2. I AM A CHILD OF GOD

    a. You are all sons of God through faith in Christ Jesus. (Galatians 3:26)

3. I AM MADE IN GOD'S IMAGE

    a. So God created man in his own image, in the image of God he created him; male and female he created them. (Genesis 1:27)

4. I AM A WONDERFUL HAND-MADE CREATION OF GOD

    a. For you created my inmost being; you knit me together in my mother's womb. (Psalm 139:13)

    b. I praise you because I am fearfully and wonderfully made. (Psalm 139:14)

5. I AM GOD'S WORKMANSHIP

    a. For we are God's workmanship, created in Christ Jesus to do good works, which God prepared in advance for us to do. (Ephesians 2:10)

6. I HAVE BEEN CHOSEN BY GOD

    a. You did not choose me, but I chose you and appointed you to go and bear fruit—fruit that will last. Then the father will give you whatever you ask in my name. (John 15:16)

7. I CANNOT BE SEPARATED FROM GOD'S LOVE

    a. For I am convinced that neither death nor life, neither angels nor demons, neither the present nor the future, nor any powers, neither height nor depth, nor anything else in all creation will be able to separate us from the love of God that is in Christ Jesus our Lord. (Romans 8:38-39)

8. THE HOLY SPIRIT LIVES IN ME

    a. God has poured out his love into our hearts by the Holy Spirit, whom he has given us. (Romans 5:5)

9. CHRIST DIED FOR ME

    a. But God demonstrates his own love for us in this: While we were still sinners, Christ died for us. (Romans 5:8)

10. I AM FORGIVEN

    a. Blessed is the man whose sin the Lord will never count against him. (Romans 4:8)

11. I AM A NEW CREATION IN CHRIST

    a. Therefore, if anyone is in Christ, he is a new creation; the old has gone, the new has come! (2 Corinthians 5:17)

12. I AM FREE OF CONDEMNATION

    a. Therefore, there is now no condemnation for those who are in Christ Jesus. (Romans 8:1)

13. I AM RIGHTEOUS, BLAMELESS, AND HOLY BEFORE GOD

    a. But now that you have been set free from sin and have become slaves to God, the benefit you reap leads to holiness, and the result is eternal life. (Romans 6:22)

    b. For he chose us in him before the creation of the world to be holy and we are blameless in his sight. (Ephesians 1:4)

14. I AM CHRIST'S FRIEND

    a. I no longer call you servants…Instead, I have called you friends, for everything that I learned from my Father I have made known to you. (John 15:15)

15. I AM A CITIZEN OF HEAVEN

    a. But our citizenship is in heaven. And we eagerly await a Savior from there, the Lord Jesus Christ. (Philippians 3:20)

16. I AM STRONG IN CHRIST

    a. I can do everything through him [Christ] who gives me strength. (Philippians 4:13)

17. GOD LISTENS TO AND ANSWERS MY PRAYERS

    a. This is the confidence we have in approaching God: that if we ask anything according to his will, he hears us. (1 John 5:14)

    b. I tell you the truth, my Father will give you whatever you ask in my name. (John 16:23)

"For we are his workmanship,
created in Christ Jesus unto good works,
which God hath before ordained
that we should walk in them."

Ephesians 2:10 King James Version (KJV)

You Can Choose to Believe These 20 Truths about Yourself

1. My Heavenly Father is compassionate, righteous and loving. (Jer. 9:24)

2. God had a great plan for my life even before I was born. (Jer. 29:11; Eph. 1:4)

3. My Father knows I make mistakes and have flaws and He still loves me. (Rom. 5:8)

4. I am My Father's beloved child and I am precious to Him. (Ps. 72:14; 1 Peter 2:4)

5. I am valuable and priceless. (Prov. 31:10; 1 Peter 2:4)

6. I'm a good and I keep God's commandments. (Prov. 31:10; 1 John 5:3)

7. God loves me simply because He created me; I am His child, His heir. (Gal. 4:7)

8. I am God's handiwork created to do good works. (Eph. 2:10)

9. God is finishing the good work He began in my life (Phil 1:4)

10. God will turn all bad in my life into good for me.(Rom. 8:28)

11. I am not perfect, no one is except Jesus! (Rom. 3:10, 23)

12. I have problems but God helps me with all of them. (Ps. 46:1, 34:17)

13. I am not worried because God is bringing the best out in me. (Rom. 12:2)

14. My Father loves and enjoys blessing me! (Matt. 7:11)

15. God wants me to be happy. (1 Tim. 6:6)

16. I love God and I love others as much as I love myself. (Mk. 12:31)

17. God is listening to me when I cry out to Him and answering my prayers. (Ps. 4:3)

18. God heals my broken heart. (Ps. 103:1-5)

19. Today I can and will forgive and I will forget about yesterday. (Prov. 17:22)

20. Everything is going to be all right! (Rom. 8:28-32)

Chapter Three

Your Beliefs, Lies, the Truth

You Can Choose to Believe the Truth

Your Beliefs Effect Your Life

You have learned enough about what God thinks of you, why you were created, and what you were created for to know that some of what you have believed about yourself is simply not the truth. You have learned what God says about you and what you should be thinking about yourself. Everything you believe about yourself is not true. Truth is the Word of God. Truth is not what others have told you and certainly not what you have told or tell yourself. These eschewed beliefs usually stem from what others have said to us or how others have treated us. Actions always speak louder than words because our actions stem from our beliefs. Our beliefs actually control our actions.

What are your actions saying to you and about you?

Lies hurt people. It is just that simple. According to Meriam Webster's Dictionary to lie as "to make an untrue statement with intent to deceive, to create a false or misleading impression, and something that misleads or deceives" (Webster, 2015).

Here are 10 things about lies some antonyms for the word lie

1. False
2. Deceit
3. Untruth
4. Hurtful
5. FEAR = false evidence appearing real

6. False accusation
7. False reality
8. Damaging
9. Creates more lies
10. Irreversible

Can you think of times when you were dishonest?
When you were deceitful?
When you falsely accused someone?

Biblical Study of Lies/Truth

Proverbs 6:17 says that "a lying tongue" is an abomination to God. "Lying" means telling a deliberate or intentional falsehood. There are many forms of lying. Could it be that we are guilty without realizing it?

For example, hypocrisy, being two-faced, insincere, or fake is a form of lying. 1 John 2:4 teaches that, if a person says "I know God" but does not keep God's commands, that person is a liar. Yet many say they love and serve God yet they knowingly have sins in their lives that they have no intention of correcting.

Another form of lying is making false promises that we could keep but simply choose not to. Numbers 23:19 says, "God is not a man, that He should lie. Has He said, and will He not do it?" The suggestion is that, when a person makes a promise he could keep but refuses to do so, he has lied. God does not do this, but people often do. What about you and me?

Then there is the half-truth, in which a person tells things that are technically correct but deliberately leaves out important facts or tells the story in such a way that leads people to reach a false conclusion. In the Old Testament, for example, Joseph's brothers sold him to be a slave. Then they took his coat, dipped it in animal blood, took it to their father Jacob, and said that they had found this coat. Jacob, of course, concluded that Joseph had been killed by a wild animal, which is exactly what the sons wanted Jacob to believe, though they never came right out and said so (Genesis 37:31-33). Nevertheless, they had deliberately deceived their father to believe a falsehood. Are you guilty of lying like this?

Ephesians 4:25 says we should put away lying and speak the truth to our neighbors.

Revelation 21:8 says that "all liars" will have their part in the lake of fire, which is the second death.

What is truth?

Simply put, the truth is the opposite of the lie. The Scripture says, "Therefore each of you must put off falsehood and speak truthfully to your neighbor, for we are all members of one body." Ephesians 4:25 NIV. Let's look at some examples of lies that you may have heard or believe about yourself.

Lies and Accusations of the Enemy

- ☐ Jesus doesn't care about me.
- ☐ I don't matter to Him.
- ☐ My sins are repulsive to Him.
- ☐ I'm not worthy to be able to see Him.
- ☐ I'm not important.
- ☐ I've gone too far from Him.
- ☐ I've not been obedient enough.
- ☐ I play computer games and watch TV too much.
- ☐ I can't succeed at business or relationships
- ☐ I'm lazy and don't do excellent work.
- ☐ I know I will fail.
- ☐ Other people don't want to help me.
- ☐ I'm not good enough for them to consider what I say as important.
- ☐ My husband/spouse/significant other will eventually blow up and cause problems, embarrass me and I will be shamed and hurt.
- ☐ I can never do anything good enough. Therefore I am not good enough

How have you allowed lies like this to hinder you or damage your life?

What are you going to do about it?

"Truth is like the sun.
You can shut it out for a time,
but it ain't goin' away."
Elvis Presley

23

Common Lies Woven Throughout Your Life

Think about some of the lies you have believed throughout your life. Do you recognize them? List them here. Dig deep and be as brutally honest with yourself. Recognizing the lies and replacing them with the truth is vital to your freedom and to walking in peace with yourself and others.

1.

2.

3.

4.

5.

6.

7.

"Above all, don't lie to yourself. The man who lies to himself and listens to his own lie comes to a point that he cannot distinguish the truth within him, or around him, and so loses all respect for himself and for others. And having no respect he ceases to love.
— Fyodor Dostoyevsky, *The Brothers Karamazov*

Chapter Four

The Relationships, Events and Decisions that Shaped Your Life

You Can Choose to Change Your Future

We cannot change our past,
but we can change our future -
one choice at a time.
Cindy Hyde

Impacting Relationships

Relationships are vital. We were created to be relational. We were created to love and be loved. Relationships mold us into who we are as children, teenagers, and adults. Each phase of life bring changes in the relationships of those around us. Family dynamics change. Friendships change, even though you may have one friend from grade school, the relationship changes as the two of you mature. Relationships are dynamic. They are constantly changing; evolving, if you will, into the kind that either enriches your life or diminishes it.

You cannot choose your parents. You cannot choose e your other family members. You cannot always choose who you go to school with or work with. You can usually choose your friends though. Sometimes those choices do not turn out like you think they will. Friends can betray you, talk about you behind your back, and steal the one you are in a relationship with, all the while they lie to you and about you. True friends however are rare and never do those types of things. You want to be a true friend. When you treat others as you want to be treated it makes the world a better place to live in.

Relationships impact our lives. Which relationships have impacted yours the most in a positive way or in a negative way?

Events in your life

We are not what we do. Our identities are not based on what we have done or what we will do. However, the events in our lives do shape us or mold us to have certain beliefs about ourselves. Major events like tragedies, graduations, marriages, births, deaths, etc. forge us like a piece of iron in a blacksmith's hands. Some of the events in our lives were positively life-altering.

One example is being violated. This is certainly not something we had a choice about. We had no control over many of the events of our lives. I love the quote that says 'what does not kill us will only make us stronger.' I know first-hand how much this can affect your life. I also know that an event like this one can make you stronger once the healing has finished.

Examine the events in your life and be brutally honest with yourself.

"Your experiences are not limited
to what you have created in the past."
Gary Zukav

Defining Decisions

We make decisions about everything all the time. Sometimes I just get tired of making decisions. I wish someone would just make them for me. Many of us are that way. Some of us may not even know how to make decisions that are healthy and good for us. We then end up in situations that are less than desirable.

We have not always been able to make our own decisions. Perhaps you are married and your spouse makes the decisions for you. Maybe you are just more comfortable with someone making your decisions for you. When I first married Michael he did not want to make decisions because he was afraid he would not make the right one. It did not take him very long once we were married to start making decisions and gain confidence in this area. Now he is very decisive for the most part. We can learn to make good decisions.

10 Impacting Relationships

Think about all the relationships you have had throughout your life. Now narrow them down to the very best ones and the very worst ones. Think about each relationship and how it has impacted your life either for the better or the worse. Write their name down on this list.

You may have more than ten; feel free to use more space for them. You may not have ten, don't feel pressured into coming up with ten different people or relationships. However many you come up with is fine. Remember this is your personal worksheet. It is for your eyes only.

1.

2.

3.

4.

5.

6.

7.

8.

9.

10.

10 Life-altering Events

Life-altering events are the things that have happened to you, that you caused, or that you experienced. It could be that your parents divorced. Perhaps you were in a wreck. Many of us have experienced broken relationships, the betrayal of a friend and the pain of rejection. Sometimes the events may not be tragic or traumatic, perhaps they may seem insignificant or of no effect to someone else, but to you, it changed you inside. It altered your identity.

1.

2.

3.

4.

5.

6.

7.

8.

9.

10.

★ ★ ★ ★ ★ ★ ★ ★ ★ ★

One faces the future with one's past.
- Pearl S. Buck

★ ★ ★ ★ ★ ★ ★ ★ ★ ★

10 Defining Decisions

What may seem like a small or insignificant decision can have monumental impact on your future. Yes, your choices or decisions all have consequences. We are taught in the Scriptures about the Spiritual Law or Principle of reaping and sowing. If we get entangled in a life of indecision we are making the choice to not decide but what really happens is others then dictate our future and decide for us. My goal with this section is not for you to think about all the bad choices you have made throughout your life, but to get you to recognize those main life-defining decisions you have made. And we must always remember that we do not always get to make a decision. Some decisions are made for us and often against our will. Try to remember as many as you can while we work on this section. Remember: This is for you to use to help bring you peace.

1.

2.

3.

4.

5.

6.

7.

8.

9.

10.

You Can Learn to Make Peace and Cope with Your Past

1. Healing can often come suddenly but most of the time it takes work and time.

2. The pain of the event is real but you have a choice whether you continue to suffer because of it or not.

3. You can reach out and help others when you find that place of healing for your own soul. It can help you heal even more.

4. Dr. Phil McGraw states, "While the pain may never completely disappear, you can find a new sense of strength and a renewed appreciation for life, as long as you're willing to make the effort." (Peteski, 2012).

5. Forgive yourself and others. This is one of the most important steps to making peace with your past.

"…take your power back,
stop being a passenger in your life
and start driving."

Dr. Phil McGraw

The History of Your Life

In this section, you will also begin working on your life line. To do this, you may need to uncover some painful memories. Some of these memories have caused you some serious live-changing problems. Some of the events in your life have caused you to make decisions that have put you in dangerous, harmful or unsafe positions throughout your life.

You will discover some wonderful memories that perhaps you had forgotten, and you will also remember negative memories that have pain attached to them. Do not be afraid of the memories. They are just that: memories. Those memories only have as much power over you as you let them. The memories in and of themselves can no longer harm you. They cannot bring shame, fear, or condemnation on you once you release them. Be brave and courageous as you work on your life line. Take the first step to completing your lifeline by asking the Lord to work with you.

* * *

Your life is uniquely yours.
There is not another you on the planet
or in the entire universe.
You are unique.
You have a history unlike anyone else.
Cindy Hyde

* * *

Your Personal Life Line Instructions

1. The first thing you need to know about your Life Line is that it is yours. No one will see this except you, unless you choose to share

2. Pray before you start your time line. Here is a sample prayer:

   Father, in the name of Jesus I ask You to walk with me as I go back into the corridors of my mind. Highlight the memories You want me to work with. Holy Spirit protect me and guide me as I search through my life. Lord, I want to be made whole. I want to make peace with every area of my life so that I can have a more successful, productive and abundant life. Amen.

3. Each number (1-43) coincides with your age.

4. Put positive life memories in the positive side of the life line. Just use tag words to joggle your memory. Don't be afraid of the memories. We can work through them together if you want to or you can go through them with just you and the Lord Jesus.

5. Put negative events or memories on the negative side of your Life Line

6. Take your time. Don't push yourself too hard to remember.

7. Do not try to remember everything that happened in your life, just the main things, like the things that made you the happiest or maybe the saddest. (I just recently dealt with a memory again from the age of six when my cousin killed my new little puppy. It was a painful memory but when I began to work with it I realized I was mad and shocked that anyone could do something like that to an innocent defenseless creature.)

8. Be brutally honest. You have nothing to be ashamed of or afraid of by doing this. And if you are, please get some help from someone you trust as you do this.

9. Do not try to remember your memories in any order, just let them come to you then write them down.

Free resources you can study.

Free e-book: http://www.self-esteem-experts.com/support-files/selfesteemfreeebook.pdf

Your Life Line
(For your eyes only)

	Positive	Negative
1		
2		
3		
4		
5		
6		
7		
8		
9		
10		
11		
12		
13		
14		
15		
16		
17		
18		
19		
20		
21		

22	
23	
24	
25	
26	
27	
28	
29	
30	
31	
32	
33	
34	
35	
36	
37	
38	
39	
40	
41	
42	
43	
44	
45	
46	

47	
48	
49	
50	
51	
52	
53	
54	
55	
56	
57	
58	
59	
60	
61	
62	
63	
64	
65	
66	
67	
68	
69	
70	
71	

Chapter Five

The Power of Forgiveness

You Can Choose to Forgive

What is Forgiveness?

According to the American Heritage® Dictionary to forgive means to excuse for a fault or an offense; pardon. To renounce anger or resentment against. To absolve from payment of (a debt, for example).

"When we hate our enemies, we are giving them power over us: power over our sleep, our appetites, our blood pressure, our health and our happiness. Our enemies would dance with joy if only they knew how they were worrying us, lacerating us, and getting even with us! Our hate is not hurting them at all, but our hate is turning our days and nights into a hellish turmoil." Dale Carnegie

Why you need to forgive?

So you can be forgiven.

For if you forgive other people when they sin against you, your heavenly Father will also forgive you. (Matthew 6:14)

But if you do not forgive others their sins, your Father will not forgive your sins. (Matthew 6:15)

And when you stand praying, if you hold anything against anyone, forgive them, so that your Father in heaven may forgive you your sins." (Mark 11:25)

We forgive because we have been forgiven

Bear with each other and forgive one another if any of you has a grievance against someone. Forgive as the Lord forgave you. (Colossians 3:13)

And forgive us our debts, as we also have forgiven our debtors. (Matthew 6:12)

Therefore confess your sins to each other and pray for each other so that you may be healed. The prayer of a righteous person is powerful and effective. (James 5:16)

"Forgiveness is what you do for yourself, not for other people. When you forgive, it doesn't mean you approve of what's happened; instead, it means you're giving yourself permission to move on with your life."

Dr. Phil McGraw

Forgiveness Quotes

- "When you hold resentment toward another, you are bound to that person or condition by an emotional link that is stronger than steel. Forgiveness is the only way to dissolve that link and get free." ~ Unknown

- He who cannot forgive breaks the bridge over which he himself must pass. ~ George Herbert

- There's no point in burying a hatchet if you're going to put up a marker on the site. ~ Sydney Harris

- Nobody forgets where he buried the hatchet. ~ Frank McKinney "Kin" Hubbard, *Abe Martin's Broadcast*, 1930

- Never does the human soul appear so strong as when it forgoes revenge, and dares forgive an injury. ~ E.H. Chapin

- I can forgive, but I cannot forget, is only another way of saying, I will not forgive. Forgiveness ought to be like a cancelled note - torn in two, and burned up, so that it never can be shown against one. ~ Henry Ward Beecher

- Once a woman has forgiven her man, she must not reheat his sins for breakfast. ~ Marlene Dietrich

- The weak can never forgive. Forgiveness is the attribute of the strong. ~ Mahatma Gandhi

- To forgive is to set a prisoner free and discover that the prisoner was you. ~ Lewis B. Smedes

- Forgiveness does not change the past, but it does enlarge the future. ~ Paul Boese

What does the Lord do with sin once He forgives it?

1. **He remembers them no more**.

   "For I will forgive their wickedness and will remember their sins no more." (Heb 8:12 NIV)

2. **He blots them out**.

   "I, even I, am he who blots out your transgressions, for my own sake, and remembers your sins no more." (Isa 43:25 NIV)

3. **He takes them away**.

   "Behold, the Lamb of God who takes away the sin of the world!" (John 1:29, 36)

4. **He removes them far from us**.

   "As far as the east is from the west, so far He removed our transgressions from us" (Psalm 103:12).

5. **He pardons our iniquities.**

   God "pardons abundantly" (Isa. 55:7), "all your iniquities" (Ps. 103:3).

6. **He washes us.**

   "Come now, and let us reason together," says the LORD, "though your sins are as scarlet, they shall be as white as snow; though they are red like crimson, they will be like wool" (Isaiah 1:18). When God washes us, we are clean. "Wash me, and I shall be whiter than snow" (Psalm. 51:7).

7. **He treads on them**.

   God "will tread our iniquities underfoot."

8. **He casts them into the depths of the sea**.

   "Yes, You will cast all their sins into the depths of the sea" (Micah 7:19).

9. **He puts them behind his back**.

   He "has cast all my sins behind Your back" (Isaiah 38:17).

You Can Choose to Forgive and Live in Freedom

1. Realize all sin is the same. When you were hurt or abused by someone who sinned against you, you have also hurt or abused someone. We are all victims and we are all victimizers. We are not as innocent as we would like to believe we are.

2. Face the fact that you are also a sinner. The Scripture states that "We are all sinners and have fallen short of the glory of God." (Romans 3:23 KJV)

3. Ask the Lord to forgive you. As soon as you ask Him to forgive you He does. (Read What does the Lord do with sin once He forgives it? Again.)

4. Separate the sin from the sinner.

5. Give the sin to the Lord.

6. Release the person who sinned against you.

7. When you stand before the Lord vow you will hold no wrong against them.

8. You must extend forgiveness towards yourself. You do not have the right to hold on to unforgiveness once the Lord has forgiven it. Forgive yourself and let the healing begin. Forgive, release others, stop holding on to what they did to you because they are not only impacting your past, you are still giving them power over your future.

9. Remember you never really forget the event, you don't need to.

10. Forgiveness is complete when you think of the event or person and it no longer has an emotional hold on you.

"When you forgive you do it for yourself, not for the person who wronged you. Forgiving is the act of cutting the invisible ties that hold your souls together. You are no longer a captive or a victim, even of your own actions. It will set the bitterness in your soul to flight."

Cindy Hyde

Your Forgiveness List

Who is it that you need to forgive? Take a moment and write their names down. Then take a few more moments to think about what they did to you and how they sinned against you. Now begin to separate the sin from the sinner and give the sin to Christ for Him to deal with and forgive (release, pardon) them. If you choose to hold on to unforgiveness it will set up as resentment which sets up as bitterness.

The Scripture says,

> "Let all bitterness, and wrath, and anger, and clamor, and evil speaking, be put away from you, with all malice" (Ephesians 4:31)

> "Looking diligently lest any man fail of the grace of God; lest any root of bitterness springing up trouble you, and thereby many be defiled" (Hebrews 12:15)

> "But if you have bitter envying and strife in your hearts, glory not, and lie not against the truth." (James 3:14)

> "He that said he is in the light, and hates his brother, is in darkness even until now." (1 John 2:9)

List everyone you choose to forgive, forgive them and set yourself free!

1. God	
2. Yourself	

Chapter Six

LOVE

You Can Choose to Love and Be Loved

Questions

Take a moment and think about these questions before you begin reading this chapter:

- What is love?

- In what ways have you experienced love?

- Are you familiar with the language of love?

- Do you know what my love language is?

Definition of Love

According to Merriam-Webster Online Dictionary (2013) love has many definitions.

1 a (1): strong affection for another arising out of kinship or personal ties <maternal love for a child> (2): attraction based on sexual desire: affection and tenderness felt by lovers (3): affection based on admiration, benevolence, or common interests <love for his old schoolmates>
  b: an assurance of affection <give her my love>
2: warm attachment, enthusiasm, or devotion <love of the sea>
3 a: the object of attachment, devotion, or admiration <baseball was his first love>
  b (1): a beloved person: darling—often used as a term of endearment (2) British—used as an informal term of address
  4 a: unselfish loyal and benevolent concern for the good of another: as (1): the fatherly concern of God for humankind (2): brotherly concern for others
  b: a person's adoration of God
5: a god or personification of love (Merriam-Webster, 2013).

What Does the Bible Say About Love?

Love is patient, love is kind. It does not envy, it does not boast, it is not proud. [5] It does not dishonor others, it is not self-seeking, it is not easily angered, it keeps no record of wrongs. [6] Love does not delight in evil but rejoices with the truth. [7] It always protects, always trusts, always hopes, always perseveres. [8] Love never fails. I Corinthians 13:4-8 (NIV)

"God demonstrates his own love for us in this: While we were still sinners, Christ died for us." Romans 5:8 (NIV)

"For God so loved the world that He gave His only begotten son that whosoever believes in Him should not perish but have everlasting life." John 3:16 (KJV)

"No power in the sky above or in the earth below—indeed, nothing in all creation will ever be able to separate us from the love of God that is revealed in Christ Jesus our Lord" Romans 8:38 (NLT)

Note: The most important thing for you to understand is that you are loved. This is a fact. It is not something based on anyone else or even yourself. You are loved. You are created to love and be loved. Even if your life does not show much evidence of this fact, it does not change the truth. Remember, God's Word is truth and that nothing in this universe can refute it or make it less than the Truth it is. God is love. God's love is unconditional. Your identity is not defined by what you do. It is defined by God's Word.

Video – Watch The Father's Love Letter as often as you can during this course. http://fathersloveletter.com/video.html.

Love Languages

Gary Chapman's Five Emotional Love Languages

1. **Words of Affirmation**

   this is when you say how nice your spouse looks, or how great the dinner tasted. These words will also build your mate's self-image and confidence.

2. **Quality Time**

   Some spouses believe that being together, doing things together and focusing in on one another is the best way to show love. If this is your partner's love language, turn off the TV now and then and give one another some undivided attention.

3. **Gifts**

   It is universal in human cultures to give gifts. They don't have to be expensive to send a powerful message of love. Spouses who forget a birthday or anniversary or who never give gifts to someone who truly enjoys gift giving will find themselves with a spouse who feels neglected and unloved.

4. **Acts of Service**

   Discovering how you can best do something for your spouse will require time and creativity. These acts of service like vacuuming, hanging a bird feeder, planting a garden, etc., need to be done with joy in order to be perceived as a gift of love.

5. **Physical Touch**

   Sometimes just stroking your spouse's back, holding hands, or a peck on the cheek will fulfill this need. (Chapman, 1995)

References and Resources

These are outlined by Gary Chapman in a 1995 book, "The Five Love Languages: How to Express Heartfelt Commitment to Your Mate."

You can access the Love Language Quiz for your children online at
http://www.beachsidechristianchurch.org/welcome/docs/LoveLanguages.pdf

The Five Love Languages Test
Dr. Gary Chapman

Read each pair of statements and circle the one that best describes you.

1. A. I like to receive notes of affirmation from you.

    E. I like it when you hug me.

2. B. I like to spend one-on-one time with you.

    D. I feel loved when you give me practical help.

3. C. I like it when you give me gifts.

    B. I like taking long walks with you.

4. D. I feel loved when you do things to help me.

    E. I feel loved when you hug or touch me.

5. E. I feel loved when you hold me in your arms.

    C. I feel loved when I receive a gift from you.

6. B. I like to go places with you.

    E. I like to hold hands with you.

7. A. I feel loved when you acknowledge me.

    C. Visible symbols of love (gifts) are very important to me.

8. E. I like to sit close to you.

    A. I like it when you tell me that I am attractive.

9. B. I like to spend time with you.

    C. I like to receive little gifts from you.

10. D. I know you love me when you help me.

    A. Your words of acceptance are important to me.

11. B. I like to be together when we do things.

    A. I like the kind words you say to me.

12. E. I feel whole when we hug.

    D. What you do affects me more than what you say.

13. A. I value your praise and try to avoid your criticism.

    C. Several inexpensive gifts mean more to me than one large expensive gift.

14. E. I feel closer to you when you touch me.

    B. I feel close when we are talking or doing something together.

15. A. I like you to compliment my achievements.

    D. I know you love me when you do things for me that you don't enjoy doing.

16. E. I like for you to touch me when you walk by.

    B. I like when you listen to me sympathetically.

17. C. I really enjoy receiving gifts from you.

    D. I feel loved when you help me with my home projects.

18. A. I like when you compliment my appearance.

    B. I feel loved when you take the time to understand my feelings.

19. E. I feel secure when you are touching me.

    D. Your acts of service make me feel loved.

20. D. I appreciate the many things you do for me.

    C. I like receiving gifts that you make.

21. B. I really enjoy the feeling I get when you give me your undivided attention.

    D. I really enjoy the feeling I get when you do some act of service for me.

22. C. I feel loved when you celebrate my birthday with a gift.

A. I feel loved when you celebrate my birthday with meaningful words (written or spoken.)

23. D. I feel loved when you help me out with my chores.

    C. I know you are thinking of me when you give me a gift.

24. C. I appreciate it when you remember special days with a gift.

    B. I appreciate it when you listen patiently and don't interrupt me.

25. B. I enjoy extended trips with you.

    D. I like to know that you are concerned enough to help me with my daily task.

26. E. Kissing me unexpectedly makes me feel loved.

    C. Giving me a gift for no occasion makes me feel loved.

27. A. I like to be told that you appreciate me.

    B. I like for you to look at me when we are talking.

28. C. Your gifts are always special to me.

    E. I feel loved when you kiss me.

29. A. I feel loved when you tell me how much you appreciate me.

    D. I feel loved when you enthusiastically do a task I have requested.

30. E. I need to be hugged by you every day.

    A. I need your words of affirmation daily.

Add Total Number of Answers Here:

Please count all the answers with As. Total them. Record the number next to the A. Count all the B answers. Add them together. Put the total next to the B. Continue counting and recording. Your highest count will show you the preferred love language. You may have two that are the same or close. It is ok. Sometimes we can have two or three higher preferences while the others are lower. Remember there is nothing wrong with any of your answers. There is no right or wrong.

A. ____ Words of Affirmation

B. ____ Quality Time

C. ____ Receiving Gifts

D. ____ Acts of Service

E. ____ Physical Touch

Ten Ways to Love

1. Listen without interrupting. (Proverbs 18)

2. Speak without accusing (James 1:19)

3. Give without sparing. (Proverbs 21:26)

4. Pray without ceasing. (Colossians 1:9)

5. Answer without arguing. (Proverbs 17:1)

6. Share without pretending. (Ephesians 4:15)

7. Enjoy without complaint. (Philippians 2:14)

8. Trust without wavering. (Corinthians 13:7)

9. Forgive without punishing. (Colossians 3:13)

10. Promise without forgetting. (Proverbs 13:12)

Love Quotes

- "God is Love... ...so how you define love is how you see God..." Vasquez Pia

- "Love bears all things, believes all things, hopes all things, endures all things. Love never ends. (I Corinthians 13: 7-8a ESV)"

- The less you open your heart to others, the more your heart suffers. - Deepak Chopra

- "Your task is not to seek for love, but merely to seek and find all the barriers within yourself that you have built against it." Helen Schucman

- "If people are going to be allowed to say "we love you" and "I love you", they'd better have the backbone to prove it. Love isn't just a word." C. JoyBell C.

- "A sacrifice to be real must cost, must hurt, and must empty ourselves. Give yourself fully to God. He will use you to accomplish great things on the condition that you believe much more in His love than in your weakness." Mother Teresa

- "You can run away from yourself so often, and so much, just because the broken pieces of you cut your feet too deeply if you stay around for too long. But then what if someone were to come along and pick up those pieces for you? Then you wouldn't have to run away from yourself anymore. You could stop running. If someone sees you as something worth staying with— maybe you'll stay with yourself, too." C. JoyBell C.

- "Tell your heart that the fear of suffering is worse than the suffering itself. And no heart has ever suffered when it goes in search of its dream." Paulo Coelho

- "Love is not some kind of a game, it is special and should be taken care of because it's the only thing that accepts you for who you are." Nathania Gutierrez

- "Many of us suffer because we think that if people don't really love us, then we will have to live forever without love. But it's not true. The greatest sense of love, which is available for us at all times, is God's love." Stormie Omartian

Chapter Seven

Healthy vs Unhealthy Relationships

You Can Choose Healthy Relationships

Relationships

Relationships are intended by God to enhance and enrich our lives. Let's see what God says about the different types of relationships in our lives. The Lord gives us some pretty specific instructions for marital relationships, friendships, and for the relationship between parents and their children.

Marriage

- Submitting yourselves one to another in the fear of God. 22 Wives, submit yourselves unto your own husbands, as unto the Lord. 23 For the husband is the head of the wife, even as Christ is the head of the church: and he is the saviour of the body. 24 Therefore as the church is subject unto Christ, so let the wives be to their own husbands in everything.

- 25 Husbands, love your wives, even as Christ also loved the church, and gave himself for it; 26 That he might sanctify and cleanse it with the washing of water by the word, 27 That he might present it to himself a glorious church, not having spot, or wrinkle, or any such thing; but that it should be holy and without blemish. 28 So ought men to love their wives as their own bodies. He that loveth his wife loveth himself. 29 For no man ever yet hated his own flesh; but nourisheth and cherisheth it, even as the Lord the church: 30 For we are members of his body, of his flesh, and of his bones. 31 For this cause shall a man leave his father and mother, and shall be joined unto his wife, and they two shall be one flesh. 32 This is a great mystery: but I speak concerning Christ and the church.

- 33 Nevertheless let every one of you in particular so love his wife even as himself; and the wife see that she reverence her husband. (Ephesians5:21-33 KJV)

Friendships

- "A friend loveth at all times…" (Proverbs 17:17 KJV)

- "Greater love hath no man than this, that a man lay down his life for his friends." (John 15:13 KJV)

- "Ye are my friends, if ye do whatsoever I command you." (John 15:14 KJV)

Parents and Children

- Exodus 20:12 Honour your father and your mother, that your days may be long in the land that the LORD your God is giving you.

- Deuteronomy 5:16 Honour your father and your mother, as the LORD your God commanded you, that your days may be long, and that it may go well with you in the land that the LORD your God is giving you.

- Proverbs 31:28-31 Her children rise up and call her blessed; her husband also, and he praises her: "Many women have done excellently, but you surpass them all." Charm is deceitful, and beauty is vain, but a woman who fears the LORD is to be praised. Give her of the fruit of her hands, and let her works praise her in the gates.

- Malachi 1:6 A son honours his father, and a servant his master. If then I am a father, where is my honour? And if I am a master, where is my fear? says the LORD of hosts to you, O priests, who despise my name. But you say, 'How have we despised your name?'

- Ephesians 6:1-3 Children, obey your parents in the Lord, for this is right. "Honour your father and mother" (this is the first commandment with a promise), "that it may go well with you and that you may live long in the land."

Read more about what God says about relationship at this
website: http://www.whatchristianswanttoknow.com/bible-verses-about-relationships-20-good-scriptures/#ixzz3jrEpMCnr

You Can Choose to Have Healthy Relationships

We studied relationships briefly in chapter four. Now let's break them down a little more and learn the difference in healthy and unhealthy relationships. You are probably thinking of marriages or couples, and those are relationships, but what about your relationship with yourself, with God, with others? We must not be narrow-minded when we are learning about healthy and unhealthy relationships. We must examine all types of relationships so we can choose to have relationships that are healthy for us.

Your Relationship with God

1. How active is God in my life?
2. What does God expect from me?
3. On a scale of 1-10, how I do I rate my relationship with God?

Your Relationship with Myself

1. Do I like myself?
2. What is my self-image?
3. On a scale of 1-10, how do I rate my relationship with myself?

Your Relationship with Others

1. Do I like other people?
2. What is my opinion of others?
3. On a scale of 1-10, how do I rate my relationship with others?

Healthy vs Unhealthy Relationships

Signs of an Unhealthy Relationship

1. You feel pressure to change to meet your partner's standards.
2. Your partner is jealous or possessive. Your partner won't let you have friends, checks up on you, or won't accept breaking up.
3. Your partner makes all the decisions and controls everything.
4. You worry how your partner will react to things you say or do.
5. You make excuses for your partner's behavior.
6. You care for and focus only on your partner's needs and neglect yourself.
7. Your partner threatens or intimidates you.
8. You partner blames you when s/he mistreats you, saying you provoked the behavior, or pressed his/her buttons.
9. Your partner is violent, loses his/her temper quickly, or brags about mistreating others.

Signs of a Healthy Relationship

1. You and your partner respect each other's individuality.
2. Your partner accepts your friends and family without jealousy. You each participate in activities independently.
3. You and your partner discuss things, allow for differences of opinion, and compromise.
4. You are able to grow and change without being threatened.
5. You and your partner do not try to control or change each other.
6. You and your partner trust each other.
7. You respect each other's need for privacy.
8. You respect each other's sexual boundaries.
9. You each take responsibility for your own behavior and choices.
10. You resolve conflicts in a peaceful way that feels safe to both of you.

Relationship Quiz

Check all that apply.

Has your partner ever. . .

☐ Embarrassed, humiliated, or made fun of you in front of others?

☐ Withheld approval, appreciation or affection as punishment?

☐ Continually criticized you, called you names, or shouted at you?

☐ Ignored your feelings regularly?

☐ Made you feel like you are unable to make decisions?

☐ Ridiculed or insulted your beliefs, religion, or race?

☐ Used intimidation or threats to gain compliance?

☐ Told you that you are nothing without them?

☐ Treated you roughly--grabbed, pushed, pinched, shoved or hit you?

☐ Called or texted you several times a night or shown up to make sure you are where you said you would be?

☐ Been very jealous--harassed you about imagined unfaithfulness?

☐ Blamed you for how they feel or act?

☐ Insulted or driven away your friends or family?

☐ Used drugs or alcohol as an excuse for saying hurtful things or abusing you?

☐ Pressured you sexually for things you aren't ready for?

☐ Raped you or subjected you to other violent or degrading non-consensual sexual acts?

☐ Tried to keep you from leaving after a fight or left you somewhere after a fight to "teach you a lesson"?

☐ Taken car keys or money away?

☐ Made you feel like there "is no way out" of the relationship?

☐ Threatened to commit suicide if you leave?

☐ Subjected you to reckless driving?

☐ Thrown objects at you?

☐ Abused pets to hurt you?

☐ Punched, shoved, slapped, bit, kicked, choked or hit you?

Functional Families

Definition of a Functional Family

According to Wandera (2011), "A functional family is a one that has some orderliness and harmony, where there is proper flow of authority and guiding rules in a family, the family will not be able to be functional. It is important for any family that there are values, upon which the family members live by and become responsible in society."

10 Characteristics or Traits of Functional Families

1. Positive attitudes and actions towards others
2. Caring for self and others
3. Accepting of one another's ideas, thoughts, shortcomings and faults
4. Affirming
5. Loving
6. Nurturing
7. Sharing
8. Becoming
9. Laughing
10. Harmonizing

Video – Functional Families - http://www.youtube.com/watch?v=jJyMEtdKDWA

Dysfunctional Families

Definition of a dysfunctional family

According to Boyd (1993), "A dysfunctional family is one in which the relationships between the parents and children are strained and unnatural." He goes on to say, "This is usually because one of the family members has a serious problem that impacts every other member of the family, and each member of the family feels constrained to adapt atypical roles within the family to allow the family as a whole to survive" (Boyd, 1992).

Dysfunction "does not stop unless we break the pattern, and find a way to heal the wounds that have been inflicted upon us, and resolve that we will not repeat the past: not in our lives, not in our children's lives" (Boyd, 1992).

10 Characteristics or Traits of Dysfunctional Families

1. Fear of: feelings, losing control, abandonment, intimacy
2. Stuck in resentment and bitterness
3. Focus on others problems
4. Poor self-care
5. Codependent or Self-centered
6. Victims or Victimizers or both
7. Confuse love with pity
8. Overly responsible or irresponsible
9. Low self-esteem and self-confidence and perfectionism
10. Harsh, critical of others and self

Video - Dysfunctional family -
http://www.youtube.com/watch?v=WZh3wJqhoKs

Chapter Eight

Walls and Emotions

You Can Choose to Remove One Brick at a Time

*"Stone walls a prison does not make,
nor iron bars jail."*
Richard Lovelace

Walls

Walls? You know. Those walls you have built around your heart to keep yourself from getting hurt again. We imprison ourselves with the very walls we put up to protect ourselves with. We do not build our walls with brick or stone or iron bars. We build our walls with fears of all kinds.

When I first heard this quote I was in Oklahoma ministering. My friend's husband, Bob Bowles said it to me and when he did it penetrated my ears and went straight to my heart. I know I had walls. I knew instantly that I had imprisoned myself. That quote was spoken to me about 11 years ago and is just as powerful to me now as it was then. I just could not stop thinking about it and how I had walls and bars in my life.

You make your own jail, your own prison with your thoughts. Think about it. Thoughts determine your beliefs and then your actions. If your thoughts are fearful, walls of fear will surround your heart that will keep possibilities out. You not have to be a prisoner!

The walls are often so strong that they not only keep the bad from getting in, they also keep the good from getting in. Are your walls working for you? Walls never really work do they? They keep us from giving and receiving the love we deserve.

Opening your heart, moving just one brick, and looking out will be an easy way to begin. You do not have to start tearing your wall down all at once.

God is with you, and you are safe.

You can let your guard down with Him. Many times when we are hurt we build walls to protect ourselves. The walls thicken with each injury; they get taller and wider with each offense.

The Lord says, "For I hold you by your right hand – I, the Lord your God. And I say to you, 'Don't be afraid. I am here to help you." Isaiah 41:13 NLT

Look at the options below and begin taking your wall down by choosing one activity that you can apply to your life today. That will help move that one brick. Before you realize it the next one will be moving too. If you only move one brick at a time you are still ok. You are not vulnerable, because as you remove each brick, you are building boundaries to protect yourself. You will learn safe habits and behaviors through this course.

Working with Scriptures provided and the Christian affirmations will help you establish new truths that will destroy old lies.

Note: One of the best ways to face your past is to begin praying and asking Holy Spirit to reveal anything to you that needs to be healed. Then give Him permission to heal you.

Telling your story - Giving your pain a voice

1. "Life and death is in the power of YOUR tongue. (Proverbs 18:21).

2. Admitting that there is pain caused by an event or by someone resembles opening the wound and digging the splinter out. Once the splinter is removed the healing begins. God has healing for you; are you willing to let Him begin removing the splinters?

3. The Bible says, "He [God] sent his word [Jesus], and healed them [you, me, us], and delivered them [all of us] from their destructions" Psalm 107:20 KJV.

You Can Choose Creative Ways to Release the Pain of the Past

1. Faith Journaling: Write the things that you have never been able to speak aloud or share with others. Tear it up, burn it, or destroy it if you do not feel safe keeping it.

2. Write about the emotions you have had or have now, like the times you were fearful, happy, sad, angry, lonely, ashamed, guilty, confused, or had no feelings at all.

3. Talk to the ONE who already loves and knows you and your history – Jesus.

4. Get help from someone. You are not alone, and you do not have to suffer alone.

5. Share your story with someone you trust when you feel safe.

6. Seek prayer, spiritual guidance, and spiritual direction. The Scripture teaches us to "Confess your sins to each other and pray for each other so that you may be healed. The fervent effectual prayer of a righteous man avails much. " James 5:16 KJV

7. Seek professional counseling or therapy if you need to because you deserve the help.

8. Pursue Creative Therapy – Art: scrapbooking, painting, sculpting, photography, etc.

"Remind yourself daily that you may not be able to control every event in your life, but you can control how you react, and how you choose to feel regardless of how you are conditioned to feel." selfesteem2go.com

You Can Choose to Live as Your Real or Authentic Self

You have studied who you are and why you were created. Do you know who you really are yet? Have you always just been the wife, husband, friend, daughter, son, father, mother, and whatever other role you play. These roles in life, or these descriptions are only titles similar to job titles but they do not define who we are. Our authentic self, our original self is based on who God says we are. We are what we think we are.

According to Boyd you can set goals for yourself. In the process of learning how to accomplish those goals your dreams will become a reality. You will begin experiencing a personal satisfaction and gratification like never before (1992).

"By finding others who will support you in your recovery, by love, by understanding, by forgiveness, by empowering yourself, it is possible to release the burdens of the past and live more fully in the Actuality of the living present" (1992).

"This is not an easy task, but no task is more urgent or worthwhile" (Boyd, 1992).

God has amazing plans for your life. He says, For I know the plans I have for you," declares the Lord, "plans to prosper you and not to harm you, plans to give you hope and a future. Then you will call on me and come and pray to me, and I will listen to you. You will seek me and find me when you seek me with all your heart. Jeremiah 29:11 NIV

"Our life is what our thoughts make it"
~ Marcus Aurelius Antoninus

*"It is possible for you to
overcome a painful past,
to rediscover your
unique individuality,
and to become more
effective in your personal life.
Getting in touch with your
Soul, your real Self,
through a spiritual
awakening, is a
healing experience,
and will help you
recognize your potential
and find inner strength
and wisdom to cope
with life's challenges"
(Boyd, 1992).*

You Can Choose to Let the Healing Begin

"When you grow up in a dysfunctional family, you experience trauma and pain from your parents' actions, words, and attitudes. Because of this trauma you experienced, you grew up changed, different from other children, missing important parts of necessary parenting that prepare you for adulthood, missing parts of your childhood when you were forced into unnatural roles within your family" (Boyd, 1992, para. 1).

For some of you, it has led you to attempt to flee the pain of your past by alcohol or drug use. Others of you feel inexplicably compelled to repeat the abuses that were done to you on your own children or with your own spouse. Others of you have felt inner anxiety or rage, and don't know why you feel as you do. You were innocent, and your life was changed dramatically by forces in your family you had no control over, and now you are an adult survivor of that trauma" (Boyd, 1992, para. 2).

Many suffer from Post-Traumatic Stress Disorder (PTSD) because of the traumas of childhood. Sometimes horrific things happen to good people. We do not in any way wish to minimize the memories you have. In this class, our wish is to help you recognize the healing available to you if you choose to receive it and set you on your healing journey.

There is only one way to receive true and lasting healing; by believing in Jesus Christ. Admitting that you have not always done the right thing - which you have sinned (fallen short of God's best for you), that you need Him to take control of the mess your life has become, and asking Him to forgive you begins the healing process. If these words are pulling at your heart right now, allow the work of the Spirit to continue by praying the following prayer.

Prayer

Father, I know I have done things wrong. I have been hurt by others and I admit that I have hurt others. I need healing for my past, for the brokenness in my heart, for the deep wounds I have in my soul. I need a fresh beginning, a new heart and a new spirit. I need a new way of thinking, coping, and living. I may not understand everything about You Jesus, but I am willing to begin this journey of healing with Your guidance.

I surrender my life to you today. I confess you as Lord of my life. I believe you are the Son of God that you were crucified, resurrected on the third day, that your shed blood cleanses my sins, and that the stripes You bore upon Your back were for my healing. Forgive me and make me whole in the name of Jesus I pray, Amen.

Note: You have a promise… "And I am certain that God, who began the good work within you, will continue his work until it is finally finished on the day when Christ Jesus returns." (Philippians 1:6 NLT)

What you don't say controls you.

What you hide controls you. Unknown

Emotional Health: Literacy and Intelligence

Bible Study on Negative Emotions

BITTERNESS	HATRED
Acts 8:23	Leviticus 19:17
Romans 3:14	Proverbs 10:12
Ephesians 4:31	Proverbs 15:17
Hebrews 12:15	1 John 2:9
James 3:14	1 John 4:20

ENVY	MALICE
Psalms 37:1	1 Corinthians 5:8, 14:20
Proverbs 3:31	Colossians 3:8
Proverbs 23:17	1 Peter 2:1
Galatians 5:26	Esther 3:6
Genesis 26:14	Psalms 140:3
Matthew 27:18	Isa. 59:4,5 Matt. 27:23
	John 12:10, Acts 7:54

What are Emotions?

Simply put - an emotion is energy in motion.

An emotion is energy inside your soul. Soul energy. Emotions help keep you energized. Think about it. Happy joyful people run around full of vim and vigor. Depressed people have very little energy and do not run around at all but rather they stay in bed, forgoing self-care and many other normal activities for a lack of energy.

Emotions that are caught up in our bodies and stored there cause us to become toxic. Remember how it is our thoughts that cause 95% of what is wrong with us? Doesn't it sound reasonable to remove the negative emotions now and allow the balance to return to our bodies, minds and souls than it is to stay toxic?

Draw some emotions you have felt in the blank faces below.

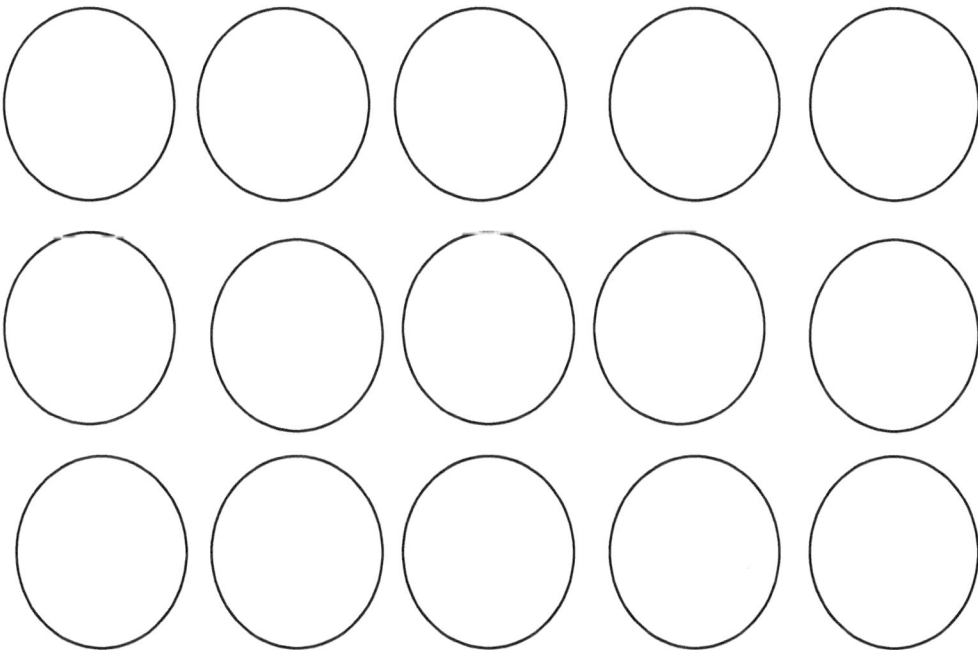

Videos that will help you find emotional healing.

Video 1: Emotions Matter
Retrieved from http://www.youtube.com/watch?v=GKK0hO0-Wck

Video 2: Roadblocks to Awareness
Retrieved from http://www.youtube.com/watch?v=nvjjhfz3oas

Video 3: Quick Stress Relief
Retrieved from http://www.youtube.com/watch?v=uxTTkc3-1V8

Video 4: Developing Emotional Awareness
Retrieved from http://www.youtube.com/watch?v=ZI4gbsTFIKg

Video 5: Taming Emotions
Retrieved from http://www.youtube.com/watch?v=vEihBsfb8so
"Ride the Wild Horse" Visit this link to listen to and read the exercise:
http://www.helpguide.org/toolkit/emotional_health_audio.htm

Video 6: Unexpected Rewards
Retrieved from http://www.youtube.com/watch?v=R2eeSs5epdE

Video 7: It is Up To You
Retrieved from http://www.youtube.com/watch?v=HE9ui5W0Qwo

To continue your Emotional Healing journey visit this website: Emotional Intelligence Five Key Skills for Raising Emotional Intelligence
http://www.helpguide.org/mental/eq5_raising_emotional_intelligence.htm

What is Emotional Literacy?

Emotional Literacy is a term that was used first by Claude Steiner (1997) [1] who says:

> Emotional Literacy is made up of 'the ability to understand your emotions, the ability to listen to others and empathize with their emotions, and the ability to express emotions productively. To be emotionally literate is to be able to handle emotions in a way that improves your personal power and improves the quality of life around you. Emotional literacy improves relationships, creates loving possibilities between people, makes co-operative work possible, and facilitates the feeling of community. [2]

He breaks emotional literacy into 5 parts:

1. Knowing your feelings.
2. Having a sense of empathy.
3. Learning to manage our emotions.
4. Repairing emotional damage.
5. Putting it all together: emotional interactivity. (Steiner, 1997)

Having counseling at its roots, it is a social definition that has interactions between people at its heart. According to Steiner emotional literacy is about understanding your feelings and those of others to facilitate relationships, including using dialogue and self-control to avoid negative arguments. The ability to be aware and read other people's feelings enables one to interact with them effectively so that powerful emotional situations can be handled in a skillful way.

Steiner reads this "emotional interactivity". Steiner's model of emotional literacy is therefore primarily about dealing constructively with the emotional difficulties we experience to build a sound future. He believes that personal power can be increased and relationships transformed. The emphasis is on the individual, and as such encourages one to look inward rather than to the social setting in which an individual operates. Retrieved from http://www.digplanet.com/wiki/Emotional_literacy

What is Emotional Intelligence?

Emotional Intelligence (EI) is the ability to identify, evaluate, and regulate your own emotions, the emotions of others and the emotions of groups.

Emotional IQ has 5 components

1. Self-awareness
2. Managing emotions
3. Motivating ourselves
4. Empathy
5. Resolving conflicts/handling relationships

Emotional intelligence includes such things as:

1. Identifying your feelings and needs, through body-awareness.
2. Having the ability to read others' feelings, and to listen to others with empathy.
3. Knowing how to express your feelings with words and/or body-language.
4. Choosing when to contain (not repress) emotion, and when to communicate emotion appropriately.
5. Having the ability to process and let go of emotion when necessary.
6. Having the willingness to give ourselves time to feel, and to enjoy the depths of our 'selves' through feeling.
7. Having the ability to lead wisely or follow with grace.
8. Having the ability to honor our own limits, as well as to celebrate our talents.
9. Having the ability to give and receive love. (Grille, 2005).

Emotion serves as an essential aspect of interpersonal communication (self-talk). The capacity to feel is what makes us human and connects us to one another. Emotional intelligence helps us to achieve our potential and to fulfill our hearts' ambitions, so, the more we develop and refine our emotional intelligence, the more we can enjoy fulfilling relationships, realize our deepest longings, manage life's conflicts with grace, and create fair, peaceful and sustainable societies.

Many of the experiences we have in childhood leave a lasting emotional impression, even if we don't consciously reread them. Childhood, therefore, profoundly influences on how we relate to each other as adults.

The good news is that we can do much to develop our emotional intelligence as adults. Counseling or psychotherapy can aid us in developing emotional health. Conflicts and difficulties can be turned into opportunities for learning, healing and growth.

Nurturing our emotional health can transform our relationships; in fact, it can change the world.

Emotional Intelligence Quiz
by Donna Earl

Below are the behavioral habits of emotional intelligence. As you read these, rate yourself on each habit. Is this a habit or behavior which you practice:

always?	usually?	sometimes?	seldom?	almost never?
5 points	4 points	3 points	2 points	1 points

	Behavioral habit	Score
1.	In all circumstances I respect other people and their feelings	
2.	I can easily identify my feelings.	
3.	I take responsibility for own emotions	
4.	I can maintain control of my emotions	
5.	I find it easy to validate others' feelings and values	
6.	I do not rush to judge or label other people and situations	
7.	I do not try to manipulate, criticize, blame or overpower others	
8.	I constantly challenge my habitual responses, and am willing to try considered alternatives	
9.	I live in the present, learn from experiences, and do not carry negative feelings forward	

Scoring:

40-45 = High level of emotional maturity, awareness and control. You have a positive and inspiring impact on others.

35-39 = Higher than average level of emotional intelligence. Concentrate on self-awareness and control, and developing increased empathy for others.

27-35 = You have a base line awareness of what emotional intelligence is. Be alert for opportunities to increase levels of self-awareness and empathy toward others, and to refine responses.

9-26 = Now that you're of aware of emotional intelligence, monitor your emotions and their impact on you and others. Notice how your behavior impacts others and get feedback on how to modify behavior which has negative affect. (Earl, 2003).

Chapter Nine

The Power of Thoughts

You Can Choose to Control Your Thoughts

1. How many thoughts does the average person have per day?
2. Do you ever think about your thoughts?
3. How do you think your thoughts have hindered you?
4. Are you willing to change the way you think now?

The Anatomy of a Thought

- Up to 95% of illnesses are a direct result of our thought life. (Leaf, 2013).
- 87-95% of our problems stem from the thought life. (Leaf, 2013).
- About 95% of our thoughts are negative. (Leaf, 2013).
- Your thoughts determine your attitude. Your attitude determines the quality of our life. (Leaf, 2013).

Challenge

Monitor your own thinking for a day. Start changing them right away.

Effects of negative thinking:

1. Slows your immune system
2. Impairs your memory
3. Restricts your ability to learn
4. Stresses your entire body
5. Influences those around you
6. Leads to more negative thinking: a downward spiral
7. Makes it difficult for you to experience the joy of the Lord

You Can Choose Who is in Control of Your Thoughts

Your thoughts control every aspect of your life. From a very young age, your thoughts have been creating the world you live in right now. If you are not happy with your world, change it. You have been given the power to change things. In the quote below you can see how thoughts flow from your mind and out your mouth, the things you think become the things you talk about. What you talk about is what you do, it becomes your reality. Your actions then turn into habits or things you do that you are not always aware of doing. Whether the habits are good or bad they still produce your character. Your character is who you are your values, your moral standards and this is what determines your destiny.

Watch your thoughts, they become words.
Watch your words, they become actions.
Watch your actions, they become habits.
Watch your habits, they become your character.
Watch your character, it becomes your destiny.

Chinese Proverb

Your Brain in Color

Instructions: If your brain were different colors what would it look like? Choose crayons and color your brain. This exercise may seem childish but if you will just let yourself (your brain) choose the colors it will reveal some things to you.

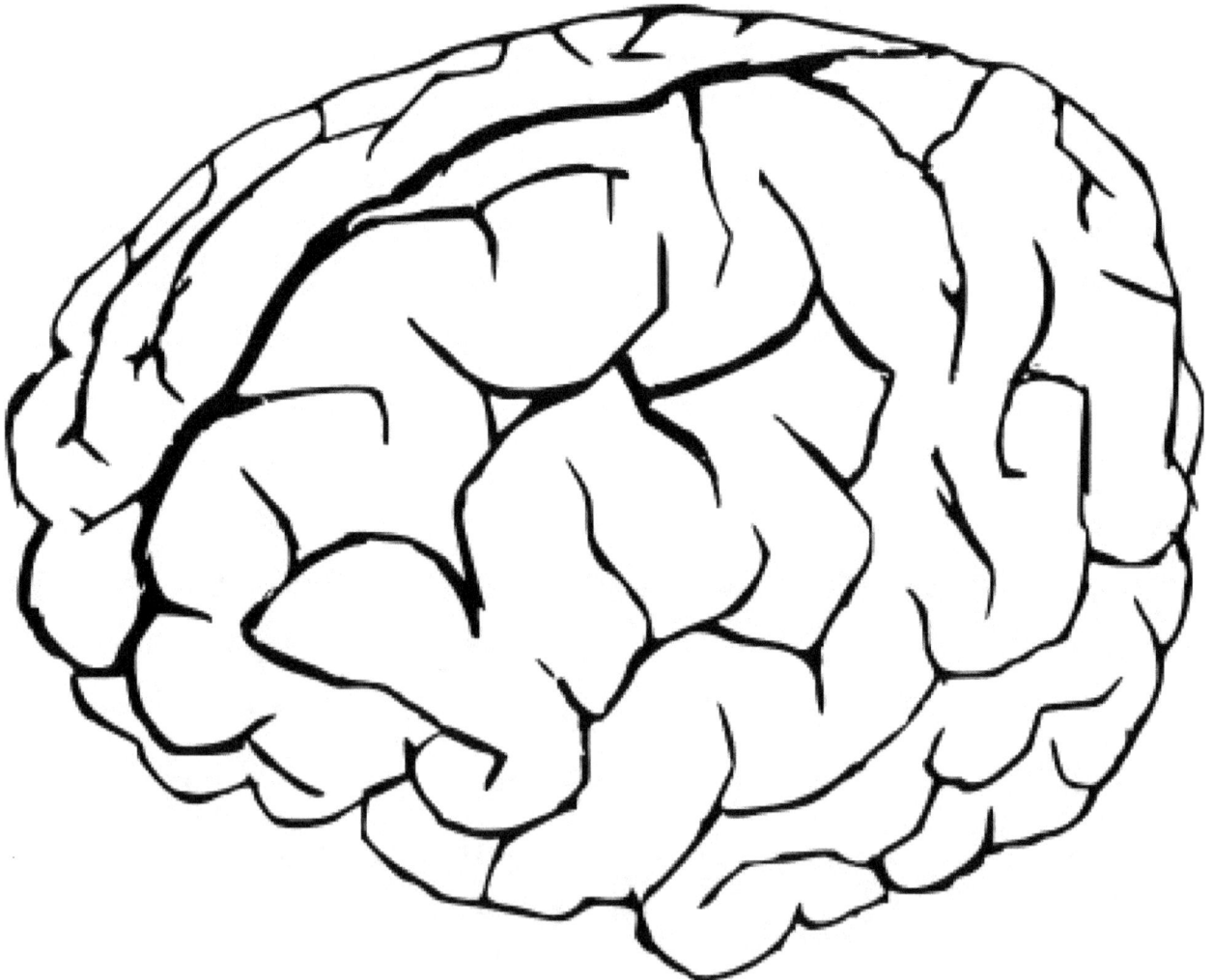

Once your brain is colored look up the meanings of the colors you chose. It may give you some insights into your life.

"We need never be hopeless, because we can never be irreparably broken"

John Green, Looking for Alaska

You Can Choose To Change Your World One Thought at a Time

- To change your life you must first change your thoughts.

- One negative thought can quickly turn into another one; then, they quickly multiply, often to the point of overpower any positive or good thought that comes. A pessimist is created when a person has more negative thoughts than someone thinks more negatively than normal.

- You have what you say.

- You are what you think. "As a man thinketh in his heart so is he." Proverbs 23:7 KJV

- Thoughts control the type of life you have.

- Thoughts have power over feeling, and feelings determine actions. By developing positive self-talk, we can conquer our negative feelings.

- We literally create the world we live in by the thoughts and words that come out of our mouth. Our thoughts come from the heart.

- When your heart begins to heal, so will your thoughts, then your words, then your beliefs and ultimately your actions. In the meantime, take every thought and examine it!

"There is nothing in this world that can trouble you as much as your thoughts." ~ Unknown

Think about Your Thoughts

This is your thought chart

List five (10) negative thoughts you need to change. Put each thought beside the number under the Negative Thoughts column. Then change those five negative and destructive thoughts to positive ones and write them under the Positive Thoughts column.

	Negative Thoughts	Positive Thoughts
	Example: "No one wants to hear what you have to say."	
1		
2		
3		
4		
5		
6		
7		
8		
9		
10		

You Can Choose to Think Good Thoughts

- "Finally, brothers, whatever is true, whatever is honorable, whatever is just, whatever is pure, whatever is lovely, whatever is commendable, if there is any excellence, if there is anything worthy of praise, think about these things. What you have learned and received and heard and seen in me—practice these things, and the God of peace will be with you." Philippians 4:9 KJV

- "Do not be conformed to this world, but be transformed by the renewal of your mind..." Romans 12:2 KJV

- "Put to death therefore what is earthly in you: sexual immorality, impurity, passion, evil desire, and covetousness, which is idolatry. But now... you must put them all away: anger, wrath, malice, slander, and obscene talk from your mouth. Do not lie to one another, seeing that you have put off the old self with its practices..." Colossians 3:5-10 KJV

- "What causes quarrels and what causes fights among you? Is it not this, that your passions are at war within you?" James 4:1 KJV

- "Owe no one anything, except to love each other, for the one who loves another has fulfilled the law. ...For the commandments, "You shall not commit adultery, You shall not murder, You shall not steal, You shall not covet," and any other commandment, are summed up in this word: "You shall love your neighbor as yourself." Love does no wrong to a neighbor; therefore love is the fulfilling of the law." Romans 13:8-10

- "But what comes out of the mouth proceeds from the heart, and this defiles a person. For out of the heart come evil thoughts, murder, adultery, sexual immorality, theft, false witness, slander." Matthew 15:18-19

As a man thinketh in his heart, so is he."
Proverbs 23:7 KJV

25 Choices You Can Make to Have a Positive Outlook

1. Love God and love others.

2. Forgive yourself and others.

3. Take care of your body, soul and mind.

4. Keep your expectations realistic.

5. Make peace with your past.

6. Be your true and authentic self. Stop hiding who you really are.

7. Dream and then make it happen.

8. Be intentional with what you listen to and read.

9. Use positive affirmations.

10. Don't lie to yourself or anyone else for that matter.

11. Stay calm, breathe, and relax when overwhelmed and stressed.

12. Keep a thankful attitude.

13. Laugh every day.

14. Spoil yourself, do something you enjoy.

15. Improve yourself.

16. Stay positive no matter what happens.

17. Don't harbor resentment, bitterness, or anger.

18. Know when to quit. Not everything is worth the effort or the time.

19. Focus on solutions instead of the problems.

20. Be good at your job and use all your skills.

21. Get a hobby you enjoy.

22. Rest and relax often.

23. Learn something new every day.

24. Be passionate. Embrace life.

25. Be persistent. It pays off.

Chapter Ten

Your Rights, Stress Management, and Conflict Resolution

You Can Choose to Live By a Personal Bill of Rights

1. You have the right to make your own decisions.

2. You have the right to use your own judgment.

3. You have the right to say "no" and not feel guilty.

4. You have the right to feel and express emotions it appropriately.

5. You have the right to make your own mistakes.

6. You have the right to be treated with respect.

7. You have the right to give and receive love and affection.

8. You have the right to have your needs met as much as others do.

9. You have the right to your own feelings.

10. You have the right to ask for what you need.

11. You have the right to change your mind as often as you need to.

You Can Choose to Manage the Stress in Your Life

The chart below provides a few ideas for managing stress. The best way to manage stress is to recognize it when it starts and change your thinking patterns immediately.

Read your Bible	Worship	Call someone	Pray
Cinematherapy	Paint	Sing	Stargaze
Cry	Sleep	Drive	Clean
Play with a pet	Walk/Run	Craft	Meditate
Go out to eat	Cook	Read	Hug someone
Email	Surf the Internet	Research a hobby	Talk to yourself
Dance	Watch clouds	Ride a bike	Soak your feet
Move	Doodle	Get a massage	Memorize a song
Stretch	Shop	Online shopping	Watch fish
Go fishing	Record yourself	Take pictures	Play a game
Call an old friend	Build something	Smile	Rearrange furniture
Go to the gym	Organize	Journal	Play an instrument
List your blessings	Feed ducks		

Choose eight ways you will handle stress in the future and list them here.

1.
2.
3.
4.
5.
6.
7.
8.

"The greatest weapon against stress is our ability to choose one thought over another."
~William James

You Can Choose to Manage the Conflicts In Your Life

1. Stay calm. Breathe. Count to 10 if you need to.

2. Leave for a while and go calm down and think about your actions and reactions.

3. Actively listen and hear what the other person is saying.

   a. This means do not think about what you are going to say to them while you are talking.

   b. Repeat what you hear back to them so they know you heard them.

4. Stay open minded.

   a. Try to see the other person's point of view.

   b. Validate the other person's viewpoint to diffuse tension.

5. In abusive situations, calmly say you are leaving until they calm down and leave.

6. Take responsibility for your actions.

   a. If you are wrong, admit it.

   b. Quickly make amends.

      i. Do not say, "If I have done…" Own it!

7. Find something you can agree with them about.

8. Visualize the other person the way you want them to be.

   a. Calm, loving and kind.

   b. Remember we cannot change others. Only ourselves.

9. Choose your words carefully.

   a. Remember words have tremendous power.

   b. Life and death are in the power of your tongue.

Scriptures about Conflict Resolution

- Colossians 3:19 And you husbands must love your wives and never treat them harshly.

- Ephesians 4:26 And "don't sin by letting anger gain control over you." Don't let the sun go down while you are still angry.

- Proverbs 14:29 Those who control their anger have great understanding; those with a hasty temper will make mistakes.

- Proverbs 17:14 Beginning a quarrel is like opening a floodgate, so drop the matter before a dispute breaks out.

- Ecclesiastes 7:8-9 Finishing is better than starting. Patience is better than pride. Don't be quick-tempered, for anger is the friend of fools.

- Romans 12:19 Don't quarrel with anyone. Be at peace with everyone, just as much h as possible.

- 1 Thessalonians 5:11 So encourage each other and build each other up, just as you are already doing.

- Romans 12:17 Never pay back evil for evil to anyone. Do things in such a way that everyone can see you are honorable.

You Can Choose to Improve Your Communication Skills

- Psalm 19:14 May the words of my mouth and the thoughts of my heart be pleasing to you, O Lord, my rock and my redeemer.

- Proverbs 17:27 A truly wise person uses few words; a person with understanding is even-tempered.

- Proverbs 12:18 Some people make cutting remarks, but the words of the wise bring healing.

- Matthew 7:3 And why worry about a speck in the eye of a brother when you have a board in your own?

- Proverbs 20:19 A gossip tells secrets, so don't hang around with someone who talks too much.

- James 1:19 My dear brothers and sisters, be quick to listen, slow to speak and slow to get angry.

- Proverbs 18:13 What a shame, what folly, to give advice before listening to the facts!

Chapter Eleven

Making Decisions, Help in Times of Need, and the Gift of Gratitude

You Can Choose to Make the Best Decisions Possible

1. Research and gather all the facts you ca about the decision you are trying to make.
   a. Ask reliable friends
   b. Ask your family members
   c. Ask teachers, pastors, counselors and people who are knowledgeable
2. Look at the facts you have gathered. Base your decision on the facts.
   a. Don't base your decisions on your emotions or on your needs
   b. The hardest thing to do is usually always the right thing to do.
   c. Follow peace in your decisions. This is how the Lord guides us.
3. Carefully weigh the options.
   a. Get a sheet of paper and write down the pros or positive things
   b. On the other side of the paper write out the cons or the negative things.
   c. Now compart the two options and make your decision based on facts.

"You have brains in your head.
You have feet in your shoes.
You can steer yourself
Any direction you choose." Dr. Suess

You Can Choose to Pray and Ask God for Help

You are sad, read John 14

You have sinned, read Psalm 51

You are facing danger, read Psalm 91

People have failed you, read Psalm 27

It feels as though God is far from you, read Psalm 139

Your faith needs stimulation, read Hebrews 11

You are alone and scared, read Psalm 23

You are worried, read Matthew 8:19–34

You are hurt, read 1 Corinthians 13

You wonder about Christianity, read 2 Corinthians 5:15-18

You feel like an outcast, read Romans 8:31-39

You are seeking peace, read Matthew 11:25-30

You are leaving home for a trip, read Psalm 121

You are praying for yourself, read Psalm 87

You require courage for a task, read Joshua 1

You are depressive, read Psalm 27

Your bank account is empty, read Psalm 37

You lose faith in mankind, read Corinthians 13

It looks like people are unfriendly, read John 15

You are losing hope, read Psalm 126

You want to live a fruitful life, read John 15

Paul's secret for happiness, read Colossians 3:12-17

With big opportunity/discovery, read Isaiah 55

To get along with other people, read Romans 12

For dealing with fear, read Psalm 3:47

For security, read Psalm 121:3

For assurance, read Mark 8:35

For reassurance, read Psalm 145:18

(Author Unknown)

You Can Choose to Show Gratitude to People Who Love You
By Lori Deschene

1. Share a specific example of something they did for you and how it made a difference in your life.

2. Do something little but thoughtful for them—like clean up after Thanksgiving dinner!

3. Give a long, intimate hug; or if you know they don't like hugs, stick out your hand for a handshake to cater to their preferences and make them smile.

4. Tell them you're there if they have anything they want to talk about—and let them know they have your full attention.

5. Give them something of yours that you think they would enjoy, and let them know specifically why you want them to have it.

6. Invite them to do something you know they've always wanted to do.

7. Encourage them to try something you know they want to try, but haven't yet because they're scared.

8. Offer to do something you know they don't enjoy doing, like organizing their closet or mowing their lawn.

9. Compliment them on a talent, skill, or strength that you admire.

10. Look them straight in the eyes and say, "You make the world a better place."

Look them straight in the eyes and say, "You make the world a better place."
Lori Deschene

You Can Choose to Show Gratitude to People Who Challenge You

11. Fully listen to what they have to say, instead of forming your rebuttal in your head and waiting to speak.

12. Thank them for introducing you to a new way to look at things, even if you still don't agree.

13. Pinpoint something you admire about their commitment to their beliefs—even if you don't hold them, as well.

14. Resist the urge to tell them they're wrong.

15. Challenge them right back to be the best they can be, with love and positive intentions.

16. If they inspired you to push outside your comfort zone, thank them for inspiring you to take a risk, and let them know how it paid off.

17. Write a blog post about how they helped you see things differently and dedicate it to them.

18. Use the lesson this person teaches you through your interactions, whether it's patience, compassion, or courage.

19. Introduce them to someone who may challenge them and help them grow, as they've done for you.

20. Let them know how you appreciate when they challenge you in a loving, non-confrontational way—and if they don't do that, be calm and kind when you ask them to do that going forward.

You Can Choose to Show Gratitude to People Who Serve You

21. Give a larger tip than usual.

22. If they have a tip jar, include a thoughtful note of appreciation along with your coins or bills.

23. Smile when you order or enlist their assistance. Smiles are contagious, so give one away!

24. If they serve you regularly, acknowledge something they always do well—like work efficiently or stay calm under pressure.

25. Exhibit patience, even if you're in a hurry.

26. Let their superior know they do an outstanding job.

27. Keep their workplace clean—for example, at a coffee shop, clean up after yourself at the sugar stand.

28. Offer to get a coffee for them, if it's someone working in or outside your home.

29. If you have their contact information, send an email of appreciation—and let them know you just wanted to express your gratitude, so they don't need to write back.

30. Praise them in a review on Yelp and/or recommend them to people you know.

"Give a larger tip than usual."
Lori Deschene

You Can Choose to Show Gratitude to People Who Work with You

31. Write a hand-written thank you note, acknowledging things you value about them and their work.

32. Offer to lighten their workload in some way if you are able.

33. Bring back lunch for them if you know they're working hard and likely haven't had a chance to grab something.

34. If you're running a meeting, keep it short to show them you appreciate and respect their time.

35. Ask them about their lives instead of always being all business. This doesn't mean you need to pry into personal matters; it just means showing an interest in who they are as people.

36. Be the calm, light voice in a stressful situation.

37. Give them flowers to brighten their desk.

38. Let their boss know how they're doing a great job and contributing to the company.

39. Listen fully if they're having a difficult day, and recognize if they need space to figure things out on their own, not advice or help.

40. Remember the little things can make a big difference!

"Remember the little things can make a big difference!"
Lori Deschene

You Can Choose to Show Gratitude for Yourself

41. Make a list of ways you've impressed yourself lately.

42. Treat yourself to something you enjoy, like a pedicure or a massage.

43. If someone compliments you, thank them and let them know you're proud of that skill, talent, or accomplishment.

44. Compliment yourself—say it while looking in the mirror, write it in a journal, or jot it on a sticky note and put it on your refrigerator.

45. Give yourself time to enjoy a passion you're sometimes too busy to fit in.

46. Take an inventory of all the good things you've done for other people and the world.

47. Write yourself a love letter. Seriously, start with "Dear Lori" (but insert your own name) and describe all the things you admire about yourself.

48. Let go of any conditions you have for being kind to yourself—meaning you appreciate even if you didn't accomplish or do anything specific.

49. Schedule a date with yourself—an afternoon or evening that's all about you.

50. Share the beauty that is you with the people around you, knowing they're fortunate to have you in their lives.

"If someone compliments you, thank them and let them know you're proud of that skill, talent, or accomplishment."
Lori Deschene

Chapter Twelve

Your Life Purpose and Goals

You Can Choose to Fulfill Your Life's Purpose

15 Questions to Discover Your Life Purpose

The following are a list of questions that can assist you in discovering your purpose. They are meant as a guide to help you get into a frame of mind that will be conducive to defining your personal mission.

Simple Instructions:

1. Take out a few sheets of loose paper and a pen.
2. Find a place where you will not be interrupted. Turn off your cell phone.
3. Write the answers to each question down. Write the first thing that pops into your head. Write without editing. Use point form. It's important to write out your answers rather than just thinking about them.
4. Write quickly. Give yourself less than 60 seconds a question. Preferably less than 30 seconds.
5. Be honest. Nobody will read it. It's important to write without editing.
6. Enjoy the moment and smile as you write.

"It's never too late to be what you might have been."
George Eliot

15 Questions to Help You Get to Know Yourself

1. What makes you smile? (Activities, people, events, hobbies, projects, etc.)

2. What are your favorite things to do in the past? What about now?

3. What activities make you lose track of time?

4. What makes you feel great about yourself?

5. Who inspires you most? (Anyone you know or do not know. Family, friends, authors, artists, leaders, etc.) Which qualities inspire you, in each person?

6. What are you naturally good at? (Skills, abilities, gifts etc.)

7. What do people typically ask you for help in?

8. If you had to teach something, what would you teach?

9. What would you regret not fully doing, being or having in your life?

10. You are now 90 years old, sitting on a rocking chair outside your porch; you can feel the spring breeze gently brushing against your face. You are blissful and happy, and are pleased with the wonderful life you've been blessed with. Looking back at your life and all that you've achieved and acquired, all the relationships you've developed; what matters to you most? List them out.

11. What causes do you strongly believe in? Connect with?

12. If you could get a message across to a large group of people. Who would those people be? What would your message be?

13. Given your talents, passions and values. How could you use these resources to serve, to help, to contribute? (to people, beings, causes, organization, environment, planet, etc.)

Bibliography

Chapter One

Father Heart Communication. (2013). *Why we were created.* Retrieved February 15, 2013 from http://www.whywewerecreated.com

Chapter Two

selfesteem2go.com (2011). Quiz for Self Esteem. Retrieved on December 15, 2015 from http://www.selfesteem2go.com/quiz-for-self-esteem.html.

Demand Media. (2010). *What is my body worth?* Retrieved from http://www.coolquiz.com/trivia/explain/docs/worth.asp

selfesteem2go.com (2011). Developing Self-Esteem. Retrieved on December 15, 2015 from http://www.selfesteem2go.com/developing-self-esteem.html

Chapter Three

(2013). Awakening to truth blog. Retrieved from http://poetkitty.com/wp-content/uploads/2013/02/Emotions.jpg

Lie. (2015). In *Merriam-Webster's online dictionary* (11th ed.). Retrieved on December 16, 2012 from http://www.merriam-webster.com/dictionary/lie

Chapter Five

Forgive. (2013). Merriam-Webster.com. Retrieved from http://www.merriam-webster.com/dictionary/forgive

Chapman, G., (1995). The five love languages: How to express heartfelt commitment to your mate.

Chapter Six

Boyd, G., (1992). When you grow up in a dysfunctional family. Retrieved from http://www.mudrashram.com/dysfunctionalfamily2.html#healthy

Christian Broadcasting Network. (2013). *Biblical models of functional and dysfunctional families.* Retrieved from http://my.cbn.com/livingbythebook/display.php?topicid=1022&id=56&val=296

Demand Media. (2010). What is my body worth? Retrieved from
http://www.coolquiz.com/trivia/explain/docs/worth.aspDonna Earl

Grille, (2005).

Love. (2013). Merriam-Webster.com. Retrieved from http://www.merriam-
webster.com/dictionary/love

Steiner, (1997)

Wandera, A., (2011). What is a functional family?. Retrieved from
http://nut.bz/2e5sy886/

Chapter Seven

Boyd, G., (1992). When you grow up in a dysfunctional family. Retrieved from
http://www.mudrashram.com/dysfunctionalfamily2.html#healthy

Chapter Eight

Boyd, G., (1992). When you grow up in a dysfunctional family. Retrieved from
http://www.mudrashram.com/dysfunctionalfamily2.html#healthy

Digplanet. (2016). Emotional literacy. (Retrieved on December 15, 2015 from
http://www.digplanet.com/wiki/Emotional_literacy

Earl, D. (2013). Emotional intelligence quiz. Retrieved on November 12, 2015 from
http://www.donnaearltraining.com/Articles/EmotionalIntelligenceQuiz.html

Chapter Nine

Leaf, C. (2013). Thought life. Retrieved from http://drleaf.com/thought_life.php

Chapter Eleven

Deschene, L. 50 ways to show gratitude for the people in your life. Retrieved August
25, 2015. from http://tinybuddha.com/blog/50-ways-to-show-gratitude-for-
the-people-in-your-life/

Contact the Author

If you would like to invite Cindy Hyde to teach this course, or any part of it at your church, home group, or organization please use the contact information below.

Cindy Hyde

407 E. Hospital St.
Nacogdoches, TX 75961

936-569-7729

cindylhyde@gmail.com

www.cindyhyde.com

Other books by Cindy Hyde

A Woman of Acts
Flames of Change
Wisdoms from the Heart
Prisoners of War Shackled No More
Beyond Abuse: A Journey of Restoration
Making Peace With Your Past One Choice At A Time

www.ingramcontent.com/pod-product-compliance
Lightning Source LLC
LaVergne TN
LVHW081333060426

835513LV00014B/1279